THE POETICS OF DANTE'S *PARADISO*

Traditional readings of Dante's *Paradiso* have largely considered this third cantica of the *Commedia* as a poem apart. It deals with those blessed souls in Paradise who are free of sin and beyond punishment, in contrast to the sinners in the previous two cantica, and is thus no longer based on the principle of *contrapasso*. At the literal level this is true in that all the characters one encounters are either those who have been saved, religious leaders, or saints. However, at the allegorical level, as Massimo Verdicchio argues in *The Poetics of Dante's Paradiso*, the blessed souls still have something to hide, something shameful in their past earthly life, which is revealed nonetheless.

In this book, Verdicchio provides a canto-by-canto analysis of *Paradiso*. He maintains that the cantica can allegorically be seen as a commentary on the political and religious establishment, framed as the punitive action of the DXV announced at the end of *Purgatorio*, denouncing the illicit and destructive alliance between the House of Anjou and the Church. Verdicchio focuses on the relationship that Dante establishes among the ten heavens, into which the poet divides the cantica and their equivalent in the Arts and Sciences of the Trivium and Quadrivium, as outlined in the *Convivio*. This approach provides the key to interpreting the cantos and the discourse of the inhabitants of Paradise who appear, on the surface, blameless. However, it is the earthly and human side of the blessed souls that captures Dante's attention, and this dichotomy is revealed in his characterization of the heavens. Poetic allegory and irony are the two principal modes of this cantica, and the source of much of its comedic complexity. As one of the characters puts it, in Heaven 'we do not repent but we smile.' A highly original and comprehensive reading, *The Poetics of Dante's Paradiso* demonstrates that the intricacies of Dante's text reveal subversive undercurrents and a subtle irony, employed to deliver a critique of the Church and Empire of his own time.

MASSIMO VERDICCHIO is a professor in the Department of Modern Languages and Cultural Studies at the University of Alberta.

MASSIMO VERDICCHIO

The Poetics of Dante's *Paradiso*

UNIVERSITY OF TORONTO PRESS
Toronto Buffalo London

© University of Toronto Press 2010
Toronto Buffalo London
utorontopress.com

Reprinted in paperback 2022

ISBN 978-1-4426-4119-8 (cloth)
ISBN 978-1-4875-2630-6 (paper)

Publication cataloguing information is available from Library and Archives Canada.

This book has been published with the assistance of a grant from the Istituto Italiano per gli Studi Filosofici.

We wish to acknowledge the land on which the University of Toronto Press operates. This land is the traditional territory of the Wendat, the Anishnaabeg, the Haudenosaunee, the Métis, and the Mississaugas of the Credit First Nation.

University of Toronto Press acknowledges the financial support of the Government of Canada, the Canada Council for the Arts, and the Ontario Arts Council, an agency of the Government of Ontario, for its publishing activities.

*To Antonio Gargano
and the
Istituto Italiano per gli Studi Filosofici
with gratitude*

Contents

Preface and Acknowledgments   ix
Notes on the Texts   xi

Introduction   3
Prologue I   DXV and *Paradiso*   6
Prologue II   The Poetics of *Paradiso*   12
Chapter 1   Heaven of the Moon: Grammar (II–IV)   23
Chapter 2   Heaven of Mercury: Dialectics (V–VII)   36
Chapter 3   Heaven of Venus: Rhetoric (VIII–IX)   46
Chapter 4   Heaven of the Sun: Arithmetic (X–XIV)   59
Chapter 5   Heaven of Mars: Music (XV–XVII)   77
Chapter 6   Heaven of Jupiter: Geometry (XVIII–XX)   108
Chapter 7   Heaven of Saturn: Astronomy (XXI–XXII)   116
Chapter 8   Fixed Stars: Physics and Metaphysics (XXIV–XXVII)   124
Chapter 9   Primum Mobile: Moral Philosophy (XXVII–XXIX)   146
Chapter 10   Empyrean: Theology (XXX–XXXIII)   161
Conclusions   170

Index   175

Preface and Acknowledgments

To attempt a reading of Dante's *Paradiso*, as most Dante scholars know, is a daunting task, and I would not have undertaken it if it had not been for Antonio Gargano, director of the Italian Institute for Philosophical Studies of Naples, who read my first book on Dante, *Of Dissimulation: Allegory and Irony in Dante's Commedia*, now titled *Reading Dante Reading*, and liked it so much he thought I should complete the task by writing a book on the *Paradiso*. I was flattered by his reaction, but the idea of writing on this *cantica* did not really appeal to me. I thought, like most people, that the *Paradiso* was not as interesting as the *Inferno* and *Purgatory*, because it dealt with souls that have already achieved eternal bliss and thus not much could be said in the way of critical analysis. I thought this third cantica was mainly a vehicle for Dante's ideas, which the poet had expressed in prose, and, perhaps better, elsewhere. In short, like most readers, I thought I did not need to know the *Paradiso* to be able to say I had read Dante.

The reason I decided to give it a try was to test my own reading of the *Commedia*, which I had discussed in *Of Dissimulation*, based on an analysis of key cantos from all three cantica. I felt I already had a start because in my reading of the DXV prophecy, which Beatrice makes at the end of *Purgatory*, I had indicated that this was Dante's allegorical way of announcing the theme of the next cantica, *Paradiso*, as a critique of Church and Empire. When I republished *Of Dissimulation* as *Reading Dante Reading*, I took out the two chapters on the *Paradiso*, substantially revised them, and included them in this volume as Prologues I and II. All that was left for me to do was to read the rest of the *Paradiso* based on the results of my previous analyses, as a test of my general reading of the *Commedia*.

What made a difference to my reading of the *Paradiso* was its division in heavens according to the distinction of the Liberal Arts and Sciences in Trivium and Quadrivium, which Dante outlines in the *Convivio*. If Dante had chosen to name the divisions of the *Paradiso* according to these heavens, which he so painstakingly describes in the earlier treatise, their relevance must also extend to this cantica. Once I began to read the cantos in terms of how each heaven is characterized, it became clear to me how the two complemented each other and how the description of the heavens made possible a better understanding of the cantos.

Although the blessed souls in *Paradiso* are saved, it was their past life on earth that was under scrutiny, and their double status required on Dante's part the use of a very subtle irony, which, while upholding their status as blessed souls, exposed their earthly flaws. Once this became apparent to me, the *Paradiso* became a sheer joy to read. As Folquet of Marseille declares, in *Paradiso* there is no punishment, only a smile, an ironic smile that serves as *contrapasso* for these souls: 'Non però qui si pente, ma si ride' [Here we don't repent, but we smile] (*Par.* IX, 103). The *Paradiso* is probably the most comical of the three cantica. Dante's humour is at its highest when dealing with these souls, which he treats with the highest regard but also with the highest irony. The encounter with St Peter in the heaven of Fixed Stars is the apex of this humour. Of course, there is also a lot at stake, and the subject matter of the corrupt state of Church and Empire is a very serious subject for Dante, but his genius allows the reader to enjoy the poem while learning his lesson. This is why my deepest gratitude goes to Antonio Gargano, and why I dedicate this book to him and to the Istituto Italiano per gli Studi Filosofici.

I would also like to thank Patrick King, my very talented son-in-law, who put together the amazing front cover of the book. My thanks also go to Anne Laughlin, the managing editor, and to Patricia Thorvaldson, copy editor, of the University of Toronto Press. And, finally, a special thanks to Ron Schoeffel, acquisitions editor for the University of Toronto Press, who has always believed in my work and has always supported me.
Thank you all.

Massimo Verdicchio
Edmonton, November 2009

Notes on the Texts

All quotations from the works of Dante Alighieri are from the following editions and translations:
La Divina Commedia secondo l'antica vulgata. Ed. Giorgio Petrocchi. 4 vols. Società dantesca italiana. Milan: Mondadori, 1966–7. (*The Divine Comedy.* Trans. with Commentary by Charles Singleton. Bollingen Series 80. Princeton, NJ: Princeton University Press, 1970–6.)
La Divina Commedia. a.c.d. Natalino Sapegno. 3 vols. Florence: La Nuova Italia, 1957.
Convivio. Edizione critica a.c.d. Maria Simonelli. Bologna: Casa Editrice Prof. Riccardo Pàtron, 1966. (*The Banquet.* Trans. Christopher Ryan. Stanford French and Italian Studies 61. Saratoga, CA: Anma Libri, 1989.)
Monarchia. Ed. and trans. Steven Botterill. Cambridge University Press, 1996.
Epistole. Opere di Dante Alighieri. Ed. Manfredo Porena and Mario Passaglia. Bologna: Zanichelli, 1966. (*The Letters of Dante.* Trans. with introduction and notes by Paget Toynbee. Oxford: Clarendon Press, 1920.)
I have used the standard translations of Dante's works whenever possible, but have altered and changed them to bring them in line with my interpretation of the passages. In the analysis of the Heavens of *Paradiso* I have relied on the commentaries of Natalino Sapegno and Charles Singleton to indicate, when necessary, the standard reading of a passage.

THE POETICS OF DANTE'S *PARADISO*

Introduction

Traditional readings of the *Paradiso* have always viewed the third cantica as a poem apart because it deals with the blessed souls in Paradise, in contrast to the sinners in the previous two cantica, and no longer based on the principle of *contrapasso,* since in *Paradiso* the souls are free of sin and beyond punishment. This view is true to a certain extent since it informs the literal level of Dante's representation. All the characters that Dante encounters are either souls who have been saved, or religious leaders, or saints. At the allegorical level, however, the blessed souls still have something to hide, something of their past earthly life of which they are ashamed, but which is revealed, nonetheless. This revelation is equivalent to a contrapasso, which, to be sure, is minor with respect to the sins of *Inferno* or *Purgatory,* but still relevant to Dante's purpose.

As I argue in Prologue I, the enigma of the DXV prophesied by Beatrice at the end of *Purgatory* is Dante's allegorical way of introducing the theme of the next cantica, *Paradiso,* namely, a critique of Church and Empire. This is the task that Dante undertakes in the *Paradiso,* but in very subtle ways that have so far been overlooked by the reader who cannot conceive that Dante may be criticizing Cacciaguida or even St Peter. Of course, the reader is aware that something like a critique is going on in this cantica as when the Franciscan order criticizes the Dominican order, and vice-versa, but this critique is read as an example of humility and selfless self-critique, reflecting the new awareness of divine justice they have gained in heaven. But, as I will show, there is more to this critique than meets the eye, since for Dante, even though the blessed souls enjoy a blissful state in Paradise, those that Dante meets have their human side, and their sins on earth have not been forgotten.

A heaven usually takes up three cantos. In the first canto Dante gives a critique of the blessed and denounces, indirectly, the flaw in his or her character; in the second canto the soul addresses the general issue of the canto; and in the third Dante provides a general critique and condemnation of this particular flaw or transgression. In the Heaven of the Moon, for example, in the first canto, Piccarda is shown to have broken her vows; in the second canto Dante addresses the issue of vows in general; and in the third canto Dante explores the issue of broken vows, when they do not depend on one's will, as in Piccarda's case.

Dante's critique unfolds within this triadic structure in each of the ten heavens, which characterize the ten major episodes of *Paradiso* and the number of chapters in my book. Altogether there are ten heavens: Moon, Mercury, Venus, Sun, Mars, Jupiter, Saturn, Fixed Stars, Primum Mobile, and Empyrean. The first seven heavens correspond to the Arts and Sciences of the Trivium and Quadrivium: Grammar, Dialectics, Rhetoric, Arithmetic, Music, Geometry, and Astronomy. The Fixed Stars correspond to Physics and Metaphysics, the Primum Mobile to Moral Philosophy, and the Empyrean to Theology. The relation between the episodes and the corresponding heavens and sciences is not casual, as it s often thought, but provides a key to how the cantos should be read.[1] For instance, in the Heaven of the Moon, the reader is made aware of Piccarda Donati's flaw by Dante's explanation of moon spots; as the light of the sun only partly shines on the moon, so the light of truth only partly shines on Piccarda's speech. In addition to the ten chapters, there are two prologues, which serve as prefaces on the prophecy of the DXV and on the general poetics of *Paradiso*, respectively.[2]

The two prologue chapters are supported by notes, but there are very few in the rest of the chapters. Although there have been very many good books on the *Paradiso*, no work, to my knowledge, has ever

---

1 One exception is Giuseppe Mazzotta, who discusses the importance of the heavens in *Dante's Vision and the Circle of Knowledge* (Princeton, NJ: Princeton University Press, 1993). Mazzotta, however, does not link the heavens directly to the episodes as a key to reading and interpreting the cantos.

2 *Of Dissimulation: Allegory and Irony in Dante's Commedia*, now out of print, has been reprinted as *Reading Dante Reading* (Edmonton: University of Alberta/M.V. Dimic Research Institute, 2008). The two chapters on the *Paradiso*, which appear here as Prologues I and II, but substantially revised, were initially part of my former study, and were replaced in the new reprinted version with one essay on Brunetto Latini, an improved version of a paper previously published in *Quaderni d'Italianistica*, and one essay, never published, on Pier delle Vigne.

approached the cantica quite from the same critical perspective that I present here. For this reason, rather than having to acknowledge the many works and critics who have written something similar but reached different conclusions, I decided to limit references to the commentaries of Natalino Sapegno and Charles Singleton. This choice is quite personal and arbitrary. Although I am well aware that there are many other commentaries that would have done just as well, if not better, I have chosen these two for the sake of convenience and because I am most familiar with them. As repositories of years, if not centuries, of Dante scholarship, both in Italy and in North America, they provide a general sense of how a passage has been read, and how my reading differs from what has always been proposed. This said, I would like to acknowledge the work done by present-day Dante scholarship, which my research implicitly takes into account, and without which I could not have written this book. The main objective of this study is to add one more voice to the centuries-old debate on the *Paradiso*, in the hope of widening our collective understanding of the depths and complexities of Dante's *Commedia*.

Prologue I

DXV and *Paradiso*

The *Purgatory* ends with a final allegory of a harlot conniving with a giant, which is meant to exemplify the aberrant political alliance between the House of France and the Papacy, which Dante condemns. The event occasions a prophecy, made by Beatrice in no uncertain terms, of a DXV who will come to kill them both and restore order:

> *ch'io veggio certamente,* e però il narro,
>   a darne tempo già stelle propinque,
>   secure d'ogn' intoppo e d'ogni sbarro,
> nel quale *un cinquecento diece e cinque,*
>   messo di Dio, anciderà la fuia
>   con quel gigante che con lei delinque.
>   (*Purg.* XXXIII, 40–5; emphasis mine)

[*I see with certainty*, and therefore I foretell that stars, already close at hand, free from obstacle and hindrance, will bring about a time in which a messenger of God, a *Five Hundred, Ten, and Five,* shall slay the thievish woman, with that giant who coverts with her.]

The avenging action of the DXV is meant to be quick and without bloodshed:

> ma tosto fier li fatti le Naiade
>   che solveranno questo enigma forte
>   sanza danno di pecore o di biade.
>   (*Purg.* XXXXIII, 49–51)

[but this difficult enigma will be resolved as quickly as the Naiads, but without loss of flock or harvest.]

The DXV is meant to be a messenger of God who will bring justice and order to the present-day corrupt state of the Church and restore the balance between Church and Empire that the present political situation has brought into disarray. The identity of this messenger, however, is less clear. By general consensus, the choice usually falls on Henry VII of Luxemburg, who seems to have been Dante's choice for the strong leader that could redress Italy's fate.[1] The only problem with this solution is that Henry VII could never have fulfilled the prophecy because by this time he was already dead.[2] Unless we believe that Dante wrote the canto when Henry VII was still alive and never thought of changing it later, we must look for answers elsewhere.

Another reason for being skeptical about the choice of Henry VII is the absolute certainty with which Beatrice prophesies the coming of the DXV. Statements such as 'io veggio certamente' [I see with certainty] and 'secure d'ogn' intoppo e d'ogni sbarro' [free from obstacle and hindrance] are more than just promises; they leave no doubt as to the quick (tosto) and certain realization of the DXV's punishment. If we grant to Beatrice the power to interpret God's Will and His future plans, as we should, then her ability to know and predict the future with certainty would exclude the possibility of Henry VII as DXV, or any other major figure. It is hard to believe that Beatrice could announce his certain coming when the event could not, as in Henry VII's case, ever take place. We should either look elsewhere for the identity of the DXV, or risk putting into question the validity of Beatrice's word, or even Dante's.

A possible clue to the identity of the DXV might be found in the fact that, as some critics have suggested, the DXV proposed by Beatrice at the end of *Purgatory* XXXIII must necessarily be linked to the earlier prophecy of the Veltro made at the beginning of the *Commedia* in *Inferno* I. This is the view, for example, of R.E. Kaske, who in a well-known essay has given us one of the most interesting and imaginative accounts of these two baffling riddles.[3] Kaske suggests that the DXV is probably

---

1 See, for instance, Jean Pepin, *Dante et la Tradition de l'Allegorie* (Montreal: Institut d'études médiévales, 1970), 151.
2 See the chapter 'Henry VII of Luxemburg' in Part I of Donna Mancusi-Ungaro, *Dante and the Empire* (New York: Peter Lang, 1987), 87.
3 R.E. Kaske, 'Dante's DXV and Veltro,' *Traditio*, 17 (1961), 185–254.

an allusion to the two natures of Christ: the human (U) and the divine (D), with a direct reference to Christ (X); and that the coming of the DXV looks forward to the second coming of Christ, who will defeat the giant, the Antichrist. Kaske's most valuable contribution is in the connection he establishes between the DXV and the Veltro riddles. In his view the explanation of one is necessarily linked to the other. The two prophecies have in common the fact that they appear at key moments in the narrative of the poem. The prophecy of the Veltro is a solution to the threat presented by the she-wolf who hinders the initial journey of the pilgrim; the DXV is in answer to the great concern caused by the apocalyptic vision in the last allegorical cantos of *Purgatory* on the state of Church and Empire. In both cases the riddle promises the intervention of an extraordinary person capable of resolving social, political, and religious conflict.[4] Having determined the identity of the DXV, Kaske is able, thus, to deduce the identity of the Veltro.

In my own case, however, since I believe I have shown satisfactorily in *Reading Dante Reading* that the Veltro is another name for the poem we are about to read, the numerical reference which conceals the identity of the DXV, namely 515, has to be a reference to the lines of the *Commedia*. If we count, from the beginning of the *Commedia*, 515 lines, we arrive at line 101 of *Inferno* IV, where Dante refers, indirectly, to himself as one of the six great poets of all time, with Homer, Horace, Ovid, Lucan, and Virgil: 'ch'e' sì mi fecer de la loro schiera,/ sì *ch'io fui sesto* tra cotanto senno' [for they made me one of their company, so that *I was sixth* amid so much wisdom] (*Inf.* IV, 101–2; emphasis mine). In other words, the reference to the DXV is Dante's indirect way of referring to himself and to his dual function as poet and wise man (saggio), a role that he has had throughout *Inferno* and *Purgatory*, and which he has again in *Paradiso* as DXV. It is both as poet and wise man that Dante will be able to fulfil Beatrice's prophecy by revealing and denouncing the greed behind the corruption and decline of Church and Empire. The DXV is meant as a poetical intervention which will be as effective as the revenge of the Naiads but will cause no physical damage: 'sanza danno di pecore o di biade' [without loss of flocks or harvest] (*Purg.* XXXIII, 51).

From the context of Beatrice's prophecy it is clear that what is at stake is not just the arrival of a long-awaited leader but a series of events that the pilgrim must note down and imprint on the memory of his readers:

---

4 See, in particular, Kaske, 192–8.

> *Tu nota; e sì come da me son porte,*
> * così queste parole segna a' vivi*
> * del viver ch' è un correre alla morte.*
>   (*Purg.* XXXIII, 52–4; emphasis mine)

[*You take note*, and just as these words are uttered by me, so teach them to the living whose life is a race toward death.]

Beatrice's words to Dante are also his words to the readers who are supposed to heed and treasure what will be revealed to them, namely, the present corrupt state of the Church alluded to in the lines of the twice-robbed tree.

> E aggi a mente, quando tu le scrivi,
>   di non celar qual hai vista la pianta
>   ch' è or due volte dirubata quivi.
>   (*Purg.* XXXIII, 55–7)

[And keep in mind, when you write, not to hide what you have seen of the tree which here has been robbed twice over.]

After reviewing and judging his own poetic past, and an entire poetic tradition, for the purpose of re-examining the role and ethical function of poetry in *Purgatory* (a subject he began treating in the *Convivio*), Dante now takes up an issue that similarly preoccupied him in *Monarchia*.[5] But whereas, in this work, Dante was more concerned with exalting the Monarch and his role as figurehead of the Empire and of mankind, and with delineating the role the Church ought to have with respect to the Monarchy, when he found himself in exile having lost any hope of ever returning to Florence, his views radically changed into a critique of the Church and the Monarchy, and of how they had both failed mankind and their divine mandate.

---

5 Speculation abounds as to when *Monarchia* was written. Today scholars seem to believe that it belongs to Dante's later years when he had already begun *Paradiso* or just finished it. One reason for this view is that these two works are thematically very similar. The tendency is to believe that after having formulated his views poetically in *Paradiso*, Dante might have wished to restate them in Latin prose and in a scientific treatise to give them more credibility. This view depends on a superficial reading of *Paradiso*. A closer reading of the cantica shows that this is not the case, and that, on the contrary, the *Paradiso* has to be read as a critique of the *Monarchia*.

The importance of a correct identification of the Veltro with the *Commedia*, and of the DXV with Dante, is not limited to the thematic function of announcing allegorically the cantica to come. The punitive power of the Veltro, as the instrument of divine justice, is similarly the expression of Dante's poetic justice in the *Paradiso* as DXV. Cacciaguida's advice to Dante to expose and denounce what he has seen on his journey, which is usually taken to refer to the poem as a whole, and principally to the first two cantica, applies first and foremost to *Paradiso*, and, ironically, to Cacciaguida himself, as I will show.

> indi rispuose: 'Coscïenza fusca
>   de la propria o de l'altrui vergogna
>   pur sentirà la tua parola brusca.
> Ma nondimen, *rimossa ogne menzogna,*
>   *tutta tua vision fa manifesta;*
>   e lascia pur grattar dov'è la rogna.
> Ché se la voce tua sarà molesta
>   nel primo gusto, vital nodrimento
>   lascerà poi, quando sarà digesta.
> (*Par.* XVII, 124–32; emphasis mine)

[then he replied, 'A shady conscience, either with one's own or with another's shame, will indeed feel your harsh words. But nonetheless, *once all falsehood is removed, make your vision manifest, and let them scratch where they itch.* For if at first your voice is unpleasant, it will leave then vital nourishment when digested.]

The blessed souls that Dante encounters in the *Paradiso*, from Piccarda to Justinian and from Charles Martel to St Peter, all hide from sight, in apparent humility, because of their 'shady conscience' and their shameful past actions, which the poet as DXV exposes and denounces. This is Dante's law of contrapasso, which metes out justice in accordance with the blessed souls' earthly flaws and shortcomings, and rewards those who are deserving, irrespective of class, lineage, and social importance. But, as Cacciaguida points out, Dante's main purpose is to provide the reader with a 'vital nourishment,' which is the comprehension that the reader gains from the realization of the mystification concealed behind a beautiful and noble exterior.

Because of political circumstances that sent him into exile, Dante became politically and socially free to fulfil Cacciaguida's mandate and to make manifest his own social, moral, and political vision, which, if it does not please everyone, will eventually prove to be beneficial. As DXV, and Veltro, Dante becomes the self-appointed instrument of Divine Justice, who, unlike the biased justice of the false and lying Roman gods ('dei falsi e bugiardi'), or Virgil's own biased poetic justice in the *Aeneid*, is able to fulfil his poetic mandate before God. Dante's language of flattery and conciliation in the *Convivio* and *Monarchia* gives way, in exile, to the voice of opposition, the voice of poetic allegory, in the mode of irony.

Prologue II

The Poetics of *Paradiso*

The *Paradiso* has always been considered a poem apart and different from the *Inferno* and *Purgatory,* not only in theme but also at the level of poetics.[1] Dante himself can be said to have contributed to this view when in the first canto he makes it known that he is tackling a subject never attempted before: 'Nel ciel che più della sua luce prende/fu'io, e vidi cose che ridire/ né sa né può chi di là sù discende' [I was in the heaven that most receives of his light, and I saw things which no one who returns from there neither knows nor is capable to relate] (*Par.* I, 4–6). The cantica begins, appropriately, with the impossibility topos that extends to the poet's inability to represent what he saw and heard: 'Trasumanar significar per verba/non si poria; però l'essemplo basti/ a cui esperienza grazia serba' [To go beyond the human is not possible in words; but let the example suffice to those who are graced with

---

1 For an anagogical reading of the *Paradiso* as a journey of self-realization, see John Saly, *Dante's Paradiso: The Flowering of the Self. An Interpretation of the Anagogical Meaning* (New York: Pace University Press, 1989). See also Jeffrey T. Schnapp, *The Transfiguration of History at the Center of Dante's Paradise* (Princeton, NJ: Princeton University Press, 1986) for a reading of the central cantos of *Paradiso* in terms of a dialectic of history and eternity. See also the last three chapters on the *Paradiso* in Teodolinda Barolini's *The Undivine Comedy: Detheologizing Dante* (Princeton, NJ: Princeton University Press, 1992), where the author deals with the question of narrating what cannot be narrated: 'What are the steps an author can take to counter what is finally not counterable?' (167).

experience] (70–2).² This major impediment at the beginning of the cantica has given way to a lot of speculation, which has found a partial solution in a theological approach to the poem. The issue is compounded by Dante's own statement on the *Paradiso* in the *Letter to Can Grande della Scala*, to whom Dante dedicates the cantica: 'and with the present letter with a summary premise I dedicate it [*Paradiso*] to you, I offer it to you, and to you I recommend it' (*Letter* XIII, 3). In the scholastic premise of the *Letter*, very much in the style of the *Convivio*, Dante gives a theological explanation of the impossibility topos. He quotes Paul from Corinthians, Matthew, Ezekiel, Richard of Saint Victor, Bernard, Augustine, and finally the prophet Daniel, to justify man's limitations in representing a vision of Paradise. Memory, he writes, is unable to keep up with the soaring flights of the intellect and cannot retain the intellectual depths to which it is exposed in a vision of Paradise.

Dante's explanation seems to have another and more specific aim. He wants to defend himself from possible accusations from his readers, who might take his statement on the impossibility of representing the *Paradiso* as an excuse for his own poetic shortcomings. What comes as a surprise to a reader of the *Letter* is a shift from a poised, declarative tone, characteristic of the *Letter* in general, to a more aggressive and angry tone when Dante seems to be replying to possible criticism of his third cantica:

> And if this does not satisfy the envious, let them read Richard of San Victor's De Contemplatione, or what Bernard says in De Consideratione, or Augustine in De quantitate animae and they will be satisfied. But if they would still insinuate that he was not worthy because he was a sinner, let them read Daniel where it is written that even Nabuccodonosor, who saw by divine will so that he could admonish sinners, forgot what he saw. (*Letter* VI (XIII), 28)

Dante seeks the authority of theological texts to demonstrate that he is only reiterating a common topos of visionary literature. Against those critics who want to insinuate that his inability to represent Paradise is due to his unworthiness as a sinner, he replies with a biblical example from Daniel that such a vision was accorded even to sinners like

---

2 On the topos of impossibility, see Angelo Iacomuzzi, 'Il topos dell' ineffabile nel Paradiso dantesco,' in *Da Dante al Novecento* (Milan: Mursia, 1970), 29–59.

Nabuccodonosor, who, nonetheless, and unfailingly, forgot it afterwards. Dante is being faithful to the literature on the subject, at least thematically, and he is not operating any differently from when he described *Inferno* or *Purgatory*.³

The function of the topos of impossibility, however, is not only thematic and descriptive but also prescriptive, and signals how the cantica should be read. Through a series of allegories of impossibility, Dante informs the reader how *not* to read it, and what errors to avoid. Representation, he warns, is limited to what the mind can treasure, which amounts to what he believes is worthwhile for the reader to know:

> Veramente quant'io del regno santo
> ne la mia mente potei far tesoro,
> sarà ora materia del mio canto.
> (*Par.* I, 10–12)

> [In truth, whatever I was able to treasure in my mind of the holy kingdom shall be now the subject of my canto.]

What Dante learns from the blessed souls becomes his message to the reader, which will reveal many truths and will bring, in the spirit of the *Commedia* and Horace's poetics, both delight and instruction: 'to those who know the entire truth will be asked many questions that will delight and be useful' (*Letter* XIII, 33). This is a purpose very much in the spirit of the Veltro that defines the pedagogical aims of the poem to provide wisdom, love, and virtue as nourishment to its readers.

From the initial apostrophe to Apollo and his 'loved laurel' (amato alloro), Dante wants to make clear that his inspiration is poetic and not a divine calling as it was for St Paul, who is indirectly alluded to in the term 'vaso.'

> O buono Appollo, a l'ultimo lavoro
> *fammi del tuo valor sì fatto vaso,*
> come dimandi a dar l'amato alloro.
> (*Par.* I, 13–5; emphasis mine)

---

3 For many scholars the poetry of *Paradiso* represents a radical departure from the *Purgatorio*, and from the *Inferno*. See, for instance, John Freccero, 'An Introduction to the *Paradiso*,' in John Freccero, *Dante: The Poetics of Conversion*, edited with Introduction by Rachel Jacoff (Cambridge, MA, and London: Harvard University Press, 1986).

> [O good Apollo, for this last labor *make me a vessel of your worth* as you require for granting the beloved laurel.]

In contrast to St Paul, who is God's 'vas d'elezione' [Chosen Vessel] (*Inf.* II, 28), Dante is Apollo's 'vas d'elezione.' The apostrophe to the god underscores first of all the fact that we are dealing with a poem that requires conventional poetic inspiration, and that the god of antiquity is the classical deity to appeal to in these cases. But Apollo is being invoked not so much for this purpose as he is as Daphne's failed suitor. As we know from the myth, in order to escape Apollo, who is pursuing her, Daphne asks to be transformed into a laurel tree. The story of Apollo, as a failed suitor in his impossible love for Daphne, reintroduces the impossibility topos but also connects it with poetry, the 'beloved laurel.' The precondition for poetry, for acquiring the laurel, or poetic glory, is the impossibility of fulfilling what one most desires. Dante is Apollo's 'vas d'elezione' because, like the god, he fails to represent a vision of Paradise that human language cannot represent. Poetry, as Petrarch also realized by modelling his poems on the same myth, is made possible through the realization of the impossibility of fulfilling one's desires. In terms of poetic representation, this is the moment when the illusion of symbolic language is denounced and gives way to a type of understanding in the mode of allegory.

The other reference to Apollo, which stands out for the strangeness of the similitude, further elaborates on this point. In his invocation, Dante asks Apollo to enter his breast just as he did Marsyas.

> Entra nel petto mio, e spira tue
>   sì come quando Marsia traesti
>   della vagina delle membra sue.
>   (*Par.* I, 19–21)

> [Enter my breast and breathe there as when you drew Marsyas from the sheath of his limbs.]

These lines are usually read as an invocation for inspiration, which to a certain extent they are, only it is strange that Dante would choose an example of self-destruction for this purpose. Marsyas, as Ovid tells us, dared to challenge Apollo to a music contest, and when he lost he was flayed alive by the god. Unless Dante is using the myth casually, it is hard to see why he chose an example of self-destruction for a metaphor of inspiration. Dante, however, is not challenging the god but alerting the reader to the consequences of Marsyas' act of pride.

The imagery is consistent with the impossibility topos and exposes the dangers inherent in Marsyas' blind pride that presumed to rival the power of a god. The episode recalls Dante's similar presumption in *Inferno* I when he attempted to climb the mountain alone. In *Paradiso* I, Dante rejects precisely the type of challenge that leads Marsyas to his destruction. The example stands in contrast to the myth of Apollo and Daphne mentioned earlier, and serves to show what happens when, blinded by desire, one attempts to reach beyond the human.

The difficulty is restated in another example where it appears to be resolved by Dante looking at the sun through the mediation of Beatrice. By gazing at Beatrice, who stares at the sun, Dante is finally able to look at the sun, a feat which is beyond human potential.

> E sì come *secondo raggio sóle*
>   uscir del primo e risalire in suso,
>   pur come pellegrin che tornar vole,
> così dell'atto suo, per li occhi infuso
>   nell' imagine mia, il mio si fece,
>   e *fissi li occhi al sole oltre nostr' uso.*
> (*Par.* I, 49–54; emphasis mine)[4]

[And just *as a second ray* is wont to issue from the first, and mounts upwards, like a pilgrim who wants to return home, so out of her action, infused through the eyes in my image, mine was made, and I fixed my eyes *on the sun beyond our wont.*]

The simile states that just as light refracts, the poet is able to look at the sun indirectly through the eyes of Beatrice, who is gazing at the sun. The possibility of looking at the sun beyond our human capacity, 'oltre nostr'uso,' depends on the metaphor of the pilgrim who wants to return home, 'pur come pelegrin che tornar vole.' The analogy, however, points to an impossibility once we identify the pilgrim with Dante and with his desire to return to Florence that never materialized. Similarly, the passage states that Dante's desire to look at the sun is also beyond his human potential and an impossibility.

---

4 I follow here Sapegno's version of 'sóle'/'vole,' which I believe to be more appropriate, as I explain, than Petrocchi's rendition of 'suole'/ 'vuole.

In fact, the 'sun' that Dante gazes at through Beatrice's eyes when he looks 'oltre nostr'uso' is not really a 'sun' (*sole*) but its homonym, 'sóle,' which is another way of saying 'nostr'uso.' Line 54 could be restated as: 'e fissi li occhi al sole oltre al sole' [I fixed my eyes on the sun beyond the sun], which makes the happy prospect of going beyond the human a meaningless repetition. The 'sole' he believes he is staring at turns out to be only an empty figure, devoid of sense, which only states the impossibility of going beyond our wont. The diacritical mark (ó) marks the thin line that divides the human from the divine, the boundary beyond which man can only go at the peril of becoming a mumbling idiot believing he is staring at the sun when he is only looking at a meaningless figure. The error lies in man's desire to reach for the unattainable, and in the mimetic illusion that deceives him into believing in the possibility of what is beyond his grasp.

The next lines denounce the artifice inherent in this process by positing a second sun (sóle) as a reality in its own right. The sparkles created by a molten iron just extracted from the fire are said to create the illusion of a second 'day,' which in turn postulates the possibility of a second sun.

> Io nol soffersi molto, né sì poco,
>   ch'io nol vedessi sfavillar dintorno,
>   com' ferro che bogliente esce del foco;
> e di sùbito parve giorno a giorno
>   essere aggiunto, *come quei che puote*
>   avesse il ciel d'un altro sole *addorno*.
>   (*Par*. I, 58–63; emphasis mine)

[I did not endure it for long, or little, that I did not see it sparkle around, like molten iron coming from the fire; and suddenly day seemed added to day as if, *he who can, had adorned* heaven with another sun.]

The addition of 'giorno' to 'giorno,' which creates the illusion of a new 'sole,' is revealed to be just a figure which serves as ornament (addorno) to this rhetorical heaven. The passage further identifies the origin of this rhetorical play in the poet, 'quei che puote' [the one who can]. The phrase is usually attributed to God, who alone is capable of creating the sun and the day. In this case, however, we are not dealing with realities but with copies, and only a poet makes these. He is the 'one who can' by creating the illusion that he can look at the sun 'oltre nostr'uso' through Beatrice's eyes. The poet is the source of the figure of metalepsis, which makes possible the illusion of another sun and another day, and of another Paradise, as copies of the 'real' things. This is his poetic virtue.

> Molto è licito là, che qui non lece
>   a *le nostre virtù*, mercé del loco
> fatto per proprio de l'umana spece.
>   (*Par.* I, 55–7; emphasis mine)

> [Much is possible which here is not to *our virtues*, because of the place made especially for human kind.]

The poet creates the fiction of a new sun and a new day by virtue of his poetic, or rhetorical, language (*molto è licito là*), which is not possible for all humans (*che qui non lece*) because of our human limitations (*mercé del loco fatto per proprio de l'umana spece*). The poet can create the beautiful illusion of a voyage through Paradise, and give his readers the pleasure of believing that they are witnessing what they most desire and is well beyond their ability to conceive. He can do this through the illusion of the figure of mimesis, and through the fiction of a poet who gazes at the sun through the mediation of Beatrice, who is also another figure. The pair Dante/Beatrice, in fact, is the most inconspicuous as well as the most powerful of the pairs that make up the fiction of the *Paradiso*. Beatrice, as the figure of Dante's poetry, and Dante the pilgrim, the figure of the poet, establish the identity and difference that provides the illusion of meaning and representation throughout the cantica.

The next example provides another version of the doubling Dante/Beatrice by positing the possibility of going beyond the human through Dante's changing into Beatrice.

> Beatrice tutta ne l'etterne rote
>   *fissa con li occhi stava; ed io in lei*
>   *le luci fissi*, di là sù remote.
>   (*Par.* I, 64–6; emphasis mine)

> [Beatrice was standing with her eyes *fixed upon the eternal wheels, and I fixed mine on her*, remote from there above.]

The transformation of Dante in Beatrice, 'io in lei' [I in her], is reinforced by a comparison with the story of Glaucus, the fisherman who in Ovid's *Metamorphoses* becomes a god by eating magic grass.

Nel suo aspetto tal dentro mi fei,
    qual si fé Glauco nel gustar dell'erba
    che 'l fé consorte in mar delli altri dèi.
    (*Par.* I, 67–9; emphasis mine)

[*I moved so much in her image,* as Glaucus did when he tasted the grass that made him a fellow to the other gods.]

The comparison with Glaucus is meant to suggest that in transforming himself in Beatrice, Dante becomes 'divine' like her. However, as in previous cases, the apparent similarity denounces a difference. Unlike Glaucus, Dante does not become a god nor does he acquire any of Beatrice's supernatural powers. Beatrice is only another figure, another 'aspetto' (67), of Dante, and he himself is only an 'image' (imagine mia) of the poet.[5] The transformation from the human to the divine is only apparent; all we have is a substitution of one empty figure for another: Dante for Beatrice. It is a transformation from the same to the same, which produces the illusion of difference, and meaning, when it is only a meaningless repetition.

The above examples illustrate the initial premise that the divine, or what is beyond the human, cannot be represented. The impossibility topos is the basis of the poetics of the *Paradiso*, namely, that poetry, in the mode of allegory, is possible only on condition of renouncing the illusion of the symbolic language of desire. All that can be represented are (allegorical) examples of the many forms taken by this deception as a result of man's innate desire to reach beyond the human.

Trasumanar significar per verba
    non si poria; però *l'essemplo* basti
    a cui esperienza grazia serba.
    (*Par.* I, 70–2; emphasis mine)

---

5 'L'imagine mia' is usually translated as 'my imagination' (see Singleton).

[*To go beyond the human is not possible* in words; but let the *example* suffice to those who are graced with experience.]

A poet can only provide examples (essemplo), or allegories, for the reader to interpret and understand according to the degree of experience that each one has acquired (esperienza grazia serba). Of course, this is not an experience of Paradise, which none possesses, unfortunately; or one's life experience, because this would be equivalent to confounding one's image with that of the poem, just as the figure of Dante transforms in the image of Beatrice, and this would be an error.

The experience to which Dante alludes is an experience related to reading the allegorical examples that constitute the critique of Church and Empire, as the mission of the DXV in *Paradiso*. This is an act of reading capable of determining the difference between 'sole' and 'sóle,' but not in terms of literal and figural meaning, since this would mean arbitrarily attributing sense to figures that did not possess it, but in terms of an identity which is only apparently meaningful in the difference which it establishes. Dante provides a clue on how to read, or not to read, the *Paradiso* in the well-known comparison of the cantica we are about to read with a journey we are about to undertake.

> O voi che siete in piccioletta barca,
>   *desiderosi d'ascoltar*, seguiti
>   dietro al mio legno che *cantando varca*,
> tornate a riveder li vostri liti:
>   non vi mettete in pelago, ché forse,
> perdendo me, rimarreste smarriti.
> (*Par.* II, 1–6; emphasis mine)

[You who are in your little bark, *full of desire to hear*, following behind my ship that *singing goes across*, turn back to your shores. Do not commit yourselves to the open sea, for, if perchance you were to lose me, you would get lost.]

As critics have remarked, many of the metaphors in these lines recall those of *Inferno* I. The key metaphor 'sea' (pelago) echoes 'uscito fuor del pelago a la riva' [escaped from the sea to the shore] in *Inferno* I (23), and 'astray' (smarriti) echoes the pilgrim who loses his way at the beginning of the poem, 'che la diritta via era smarrita' [for the direct way was lost] (*Inf.* I, 3). In consonance with this parallelism, the lines are usually explained as a warning to those readers who lack the sufficient theological and philosophical background necessary to follow and understand the cantica.⁶ This reading, however, depends more on our received ideas of *Paradiso*, and the poem as a whole, than from the actual lines.

Dante's warning, however, concerns how the cantica ought to be read, which is made clear by that 'desiderosi d'ascoltar' and 'cantando varca,' which echo *Purgatory* II, and the Casella episode where the souls, seduced by the sweet song of the canzone, 'Amor che ne la mente mi ragiona,' do not heed its allegorical-philosophical meaning, which would help them find their way up the mountain of Purgatory.⁷ Similarly, in *Paradiso*, Dante reminds his readers that the poem is written for their edification and not just for their pleasure. Those who disregard its character as an allegorical poem and ignore the hidden sense it wants to convey will get lost. As Dante points out, the *Paradiso* is not your typical journey through Paradise:

L'acqua ch'io prendo già mai non si corse
  Minerva spira, e conducemi Apollo,
  e nove Muse mi dimostran l'Orse.
  (*Par.* II, 7–9; emphasis mine)

[*The waters that I travel were never sailed before.* Minerva breathes and Apollo guides me, and nine Muses point out the Bears to me.]

Its waters have never been navigated before, not because nobody has ever tried to represent Paradise in poetry before but because this is a poem that has to be read critically in terms of the allegorical examples it provides, which entails resisting being seduced by the 'sweet' rhetoric of the blessed souls in Paradise.

The allusion to the 'bread of angels' (pan de li angeli) once again reiterates this point, as well as the seminal role that the *Convivio* plays in the *Paradiso*. The reference is to the task of the poet, who, as the mediator at the banquet of angels, provides a commentary to the canzoni for

---

6 For example, Sapegno in his commentary writes: 'This is a solemn admonition to the readers to consider, while they are still in time, how difficult and sublime is the subject matter that the poet is about to treat so they shouldn't presume to be capable of understanding it without the background of a strong philosophical and theological preparation.' The translation is mine.
7 For a more detailed reading of this episode, see chapter 4 of *Reading Dante Reading*.

the benefit of those few readers who are willing and capable of comprehending them. Similarly, in the *Paradiso*, Dante invites to his banquet only those few who are capable of understanding his allegorical poetry and of being nourished by it.

> *Voialtri pochi* che drizzaste il collo
> per tempo *al pan de li angeli*, del quale
> vivesi qui ma non sen vien satollo,
> metter potete ben per l'alto sale
> vostro navigio, servando mio solco
> dinanzi all'acqua the ritorna equale.
> (*Par.* II, 10–15; emphasis mine)

[*Those few of you* who lifted up your necks in time for *the bread of angels*, on which we feed here but are never sated, you may indeed commit your vessel to the deep sea, following my furrow ahead of the water that turns smooth again.]

To these 'few' (pochi), Dante gives advice on how to read through the rhetoric of the blessed they encounter in *Paradiso,* who appear immaculate and without sin until their flaws and shortcomings are revealed. This ironic method of reading is compared to the temporary furrow (solco) a boat leaves as it crosses a stretch of water, and makes visible a difference between two apparently equal terms similar to the diacritical mark that differentiates 'sole' from 'sóle' and 'giorno' from 'giorno.' By denouncing through apparent identity the empty rhetoric of the blessed souls, Dante's irony brings about the punitive action of the DXV, and his critique of Church and Empire.

In each case, the error is associated with a symbolic conception of language that seduces man into believing in the reality of what he desires. Reading the cantica entails the demystification of this illusory identification in the awareness that emerges of the loss of meaning inherent in all such claims. The 'solco,' which Dante's ironic writing traces across the *Paradiso,* brings about the disruption of symbolic mystification by allegory and defines the poetics of *Paradiso* as an allegory of irony.

1 Heaven of the Moon: Grammar (II–IV)

Dico che 'l cielo de la Luna con la Gramatica si somiglia, per che ad esso si può comparare; che se la Luna si guarda bene, due cose si veggiono in essa proprie, che non si veggiono ne l'altre stelle: l'una sì è l'ombra che è in essa, la quale non è altro che raritade del suo corpo, a la quale non possono terminare li raggi del sole e ripercuotesi così come ne l'altre parti; l'altra si è la variazione de la sua luminositade, che ora luce da uno lato, e ora luce da un altro, secondo che lo sole la vede. E queste due proprietadi hae la Grammatica: ché, per la sua infinitade, li raggi de la ragione in essa non si terminano, in parte spezialmente de li vocabuli; e luce or di qua or di là in tanto quanto certi vocabuli, certe declinazioni, certe costruzioni sono in uso che già non furono, e molte già furono che ancor saranno; sì come dice Orazio nel principio de la Poetria, quando dice: 'Molti vocabuli rinasceranno che già caddero.' (*Conv.* II, xiii, 9–11)

[I declare that the heaven of the Moon is like Grammar, because it has two properties on whose account it may be compared to that science. Anyone who carefully observes the Moon notes that there are two features characteristic of it, which do not appear in any of the other stars: the first is the presence in it of shadow, which is nothing other than the occurrence of low density in the body of this star, on which the sun's rays cannot rest and be reflected as they are by its other parts; the second is the variation in its luminosity, for it shines on different sides at different times, depending on how the sun is facing it. Grammar has both these properties, for, on account of the quality of infinity it possesses, the rays of reason cannot come to rest on it, particularly in the realm of vocabulary; and it shines from different places at different times, in that certain words, certain declensions, and certain constructions are currently in use which previously were not, and many were previously in use which will again be so, as Horace remarks at the beginning of the *Poetics*, when he says: 'Many words will rise to new life which once fell from favour.']

The analogy between Moon and Grammar is defined by the Moon's precarious relation to the Sun. Just as the Sun does not illuminate the Moon entirely, but leaves some of its parts in the dark, resulting in Moon spots, Logic only partly coincides with Grammar. The problem is with language, which is always in flux, and what is in use and meaningful today will be meaningless tomorrow, and vice versa. The discrepancy between Grammar and Logic makes it impossible for Grammar to fully account for Logic. One cannot assume, therefore, that grammatical structures will yield the meaning they appear to promise; on the contrary, some of those terms that appear to be meaningful and coherent turn out not to be so. The problematic of the Heaven of the Moon is characterized by this precarious relation between Grammar and Logic stated by Beatrice at the beginning of *Paradiso* II as: 'poi dietro ai sensi/vedi che *la ragione ha corte l'ali'* [following after the senses, *reason has short wings*] (*Par.* II, 56–7; emphasis mine). This is a warning to the reader that what appears to be is not always the case, or that meaning does not follow logically from what is stated grammatically. Right understanding is predicated on the true nature of lunar spots, and on this question Beatrice sets out to prove that Dante is wrong:

> Ed ella: 'Certo assai vedrai sommerso
>   nel falso il creder tuo, se bene ascolti
>   l'argomentar ch'io li farò avverso.
> (*Par.* II, 61–3)

[And she: 'To be sure you shall see your beliefs sink deep in error if you listen well to the reasons I bring against them.]

Whereas Dante had claimed that the difference between the dark and light parts of the moon was due to 'i corpi rari e densi' [rare and dense matter] (*Par.* II, 60). Beatrice, in confuting this theory, shows that it is due to the different intensity of their angelic natures.

> Per la natura lieta onde deriva,
>   la virtù mista per lo corpo luce
>   come letizia per pupilla viva.

Heaven of the Moon: Grammar   25

> Da essa vien ciò che da luce a luce
>   par differente, non da denso e raro:
>   essa è il formal principio che produce,
> conforme a sua bontà, lo turbo e 'l chiaro.'
>   (*Par.* II, 142–8).

[By the joyous nature whence it springs, the mingled virtue shines through the body as joy through the living pupil. From this comes that difference which appears between light and light, not from density and rarity; this is the formative principle which produces, according to its excellence, the dark and bright.']

Beatrice's intervention provides the 'formal principle' (formal principio) that makes it possible to understand and read these cantos. The view espoused by Dante would confine our reading within a dichotomy of light and dark, 'density and rarity,' but it is precisely this view that Beatrice opposes. The difference is not between two opposites but between two equals, or apparent equals, such as between light and light: 'From this comes that difference which appears between light and light.' The difference is not the result of an opposition but of a similarity, which, on close attention, turns out to be a difference.

In his address to the readers in *Paradiso* III, Dante warns of a similar error he committed contrary to Narcissus.

> tali vid'io piú facce a parlar pronte;
>   *per ch'io dentro all'error contrario corsi*
>   *a quel ch' accese amore tra l'omo e `l fonte.*
>   (*Par.* III, 16–19; emphasis mine)

[so I saw many faces ready to speak; wherefore *I fell into the contrary error to that which kindled love between man and spring*.]

Believing he was seeing the reflected images of the blessed, Dante turned around expecting to see them, but sees nothing.

> Subito sì com'io di lor m'accorsi,
>   *quelle stimando specchianti sembianti,*
>   per veder di cui fosser, li occhi torsi;
> e nulla vidi, e ritorsili avanti
>   dritti nel lume della dolce guida,

che, sorridendo, ardea nelli occhi santi.
(*Par.* III, 19–24; emphasis mine)

[As soon as I became aware of them, *judging them to be mirrored faces,* I turned round to see who they were, and saw nothing; and I turned forward again, straight into the light of my sweet guide who, smiling, was glowing in her holy eyes.]

Beatrice reproaches him because he has foolishly turned around believing the blessed souls to be reflected images, when in fact they are real substances:

'Non ti maravigliar perch'io sorrida,'
   mi disse, 'appresso il tuo pueril coto,
   poi sopra *'l vero ancor lo piè non fida,*
ma te rivolve, come suole, a vòto:
   vere sustanze son ciò che tu vedi
   qui rilegate per manco di voto.
(*Par.* III, 25–30; emphasis mine)

['Do not wonder why I smile at your foolish thinking,' she said to me, *since it does not yet trust itself upon the truth, but turns you around, as is its wont, to empty.* These that you see are real substances, relegated here for *failing their vows.*]

While Narcissus' error is to have mistaken a reflection for the real object – his mirrored face for that of a beautiful youth – Dante's contrary error is to have taken a reflection for a reflection – the appearance of many speaking faces (più facce a parlar pronte). Dante's error, as Beatrice tells him, is the result of 'childish thinking' (pueril coto), which believes that an image is necessarily an image of something else, that it is referential, and must point to an object outside itself. This is typical of human reasoning, which, as it is in the habit of doing, 'come suole' [as is its wont], follows the dictates of Logic, and always comes up empty. In correcting him, Beatrice wants to point out that in this Heaven of the Moon, if one follows the dictates of Logic one ends in error.

   Dante's error is that in seeing those 'specchianti sembianti' he thought he saw 'mirrored faces,' as the line is usually translated. Dante's mistake is mirrored in the translation, so as Beatrice corrects Dante we should correct the translation. The phrase 'specchianti sembianti,' translated literally, is 'reflecting resemblances,' which does not make sense at first, but in this Heaven of the Moon, making sense is not a virtue. When the phrase is applied to the blessed souls of this heaven who have been 'banished' (relegated) here because of their failed vows, the phrase describes their real nature as souls that 'appear to be reflections' but are not. When we look for their real essence, just as Dante did, we come up empty. His error is similar to the one described earlier in Prologue II when 'sóle' (as is its wont) is taken for the sun (sole). A similar error occurs when Beatrice tells Dante that he has come up empty, 'ma te rivolve ... a vòto,' because he has employed his 'childish (logical) thinking' (pueril coto), as he is in the habit of doing, 'come suole'(or 'come sóle'). When he reasons logically, Dante no longer knows what to trust, 'poi sopra 'l vero ancor lo piè non fida.' As Beatrice tells him, these blessed souls are 'vere sustanze' [real substances], that is, they are what they are and not what they would like to be: reflections, of something else.

Her instruction to Dante (and to the reader) to listen and to believe what the blessed souls tell him, is another instance of confusion, which baffles his and our logical minds:

Però parla con esse e odi e credi;
 ché la verace luce che le *appaga*
 da sé non lascia lor torcer li piedi.'
 (*Par.* III, 31–3; emphasis mine)

[But speak to them, and listen and believe, because the true light which *satisfies* them does not allow them to turn their feet.']

To take Beatrice at her word would mean committing the same error as Narcissus. The next lines, ending with 'vaga/smaga'(34, 36), rhyme with 'appaga' of line 32 and recall the 'femmina balba' of *Purgatory* XIX, which alert us to the dangers of taking these souls at their word. Beatrice, identified as 'dolce guida' (sweet guide), takes on the role of siren leading Dante and the reader into a trap. As I have often indicated in *Reading Dante Reading* (see, for instance, the Casella episode), whenever the adjective 'dolce' is used it ushers in a scene of seduction and mystification, which turns out to be anything but 'sweet.' But the emphasis of the passage is on her 'smile,' which is repeated twice: 'sorridendo' [smiling] (24) at Dante's foolish reaction, and 'Non ti maravigliar perch' io sorrida' [Don't wonder why I am smiling] (25). We should, therefore, wonder why she is smiling, and the answer, once again, has to do with reading the passage logically, or, which is the same, literally. To listen and to believe the blessed souls directly would mean to be seduced by their story, as Dante is by Piccarda's reasons why she failed her vows. To read correctly, according to the 'true light' (verace luce), implies determining the extent to which their reasoning, motivated by their desire, falls short, making it impossible for them to turn 'their feet,' that is, to conceal their flaw and seduce the reader with their fiction. Just as Lucy is the 'true' light that saves Dante from the grips of the femmina balba in *Purgatory* XIX, the Moon spots in this Heaven of the Moon denounce the discrepancy between Logic and Grammar and the impossibility of their ever coinciding.

* * *

The blessed souls Dante meets in this heaven are never what they appear to be. As Beatrice relates, they have been banished to this heaven for failing their vows, 'manco di vòto.' Because of their failings they appear to be substances but they are not, just like their vows, which were never fulfilled. In Piccarda's words, these souls are happy with what they have: 'che fa volerne/sol quel ch'avemo, e d'altro non ci asseta' [makes us will only what we have and thirst for nothing else] (*Par.* III, 71–2), and, as it turns out, they have nothing. These souls are very difficult to recognize: '"Ne'" mirabili aspetti/ vostri risplende non so che divino/ che vi trasmuta da' primi concetti' [In your wondrous aspects there shines forth I know not what of divine which transforms you from the first concepts] (*Par.* III, 58–60). The divine light that transforms them makes them different from what they were, namely, it makes them appear to be full substances, when, in fact, they are vague and empty. Piccarda Donati, who is supposed to be one of the 'vere sustanze' [real substances] (*Par.* III, 29) is also said to be 'vaga' [vague]: 'ombra che parea piú vaga [shade that seemed most vague] (*Par.* III, 34), without substance.

However, Dante's desire to meet the soul of Piccarda Donati, to whom he is related through his wife, Gemma Donati, who is the sister of his 'good' friend Forese, blinds him, and confuses him as to her 'real' substance. Piccarda introduces herself in her double predicament of 'vergin sorella' [virgin sister] (*Par.* III, 46), that is, both as someone who as a virgin wanted to be a nun, and Corso Donati's 'sister.' Her other attribute, by which she was known, which is equally ambiguous, is that she was very beautiful ('l'esser più bella') (48). Sapegno quotes from l'Ottimo, who explains that being beautiful she devoted herself to God, 'Essendo bellissima fanciulla, dirizzò l'anima sua a Dio,' an argument which does not make logical sense. In fact, the contrary is rather the case: that being beautiful and forced to marry someone she didn't like, she devoted herself to God.

Piccarda's destiny is played out between her desire to follow a life as a nun and her brother Corso's wish that she marry Rossellino della Tosa, a Florentine, to whom he had promised her. Piccarda relates how she meant to follow the example of Santa Chiara, and how she went to a convent where she took her vows to follow her order: 'Dal mondo, per seguirla, giovinetta/ fuggi'mi, e nel suo abito mi chiusi,/e promisi la via della sua setta' [As a young girl, I fled from the world to follow her and shut myself in her habit and promised myself to the way of her order] (*Par.* III, 103–5). But Corso took her from the convent and married her to Rossellino: 'Uomini poi, a mal più che a bene usi, fuor mi rapiron della dolce chiostra:/ Iddio si sa qual poi mia vita fusi' [Then men more used to evil than to good snatched me from the sweet cloister. God knows what my life was then] (106–8).

This is all the information Piccarda gives about herself, but her story continues, indirectly, by reflection, as the story of another soul, Costanza d'Altavilla, who never appears but with whom Piccarda says that she shares a similar fate. We are told that Costanza, having taken her vows, was also forced to renounce them and marry Henry VI. Another similarity between them is in their name. Costanza is the name chosen by Piccarda as a nun, possibly to emphasize the constancy of her faith. In Piccarda's own words, the stories of the two women are so similar that what she says of herself also applies to Costanza: 'ciò ch'io dico di me, di sé intende' [what I say of myself, applies to her)] (*Par.* III,112), so, instead of relating her own story, Piccarda speaks only of Costanza d'Altavilla, assuming that what she says about her also applies to herself.

Why this reversal and why does Piccarda seek to clothe herself in Costanza's habit, 'nel suo abito mi chiusi'? What is the difference in their similarity, the diacritical mark that distinguishes Piccarda from Costanza, determining one as image and the other as reality, one false and the other true? When Piccarda tells us that Costanza remained true to her vocation: 'non fu dal vel del cor già mai disciolta' [she was never unfastened from the veil of her heart] (*Par.* III, 117), are we meant, then, to believe that Piccarda, too, by association, remained faithful to Christ, even after her abduction?

The story of the abduction of Costanza d'Altavilla, which even in Dante's times was apocryphal, makes Piccarda's story questionable through the doubling of the names, Costanza/ Costanza, which, despite their similarity, do not mean the same thing. If the name Costanza, when referred to Constance of Altaville, really points to the constancy of her faith, 'Quest'è la luce della gran Costanza' [this is the light of the great Constance] (*Par.* III, 118), then Piccarda's name 'Costanza' is just a name, and does not imply constancy of faith. In fact, the point of the reversal is to make the reader believe that Piccarda, too, was constant in her love of Christ, but as we find out in the next canto, she was not. As most commentators have remarked, Piccarda was never serious about becoming a nun, as she claims. She had run away to a convent only because she did not want to marry Rossellino. The analogy with Costanza conceals precisely the fact that Piccarda was not constant in her vows, but it only appears as if she were. Another way of stating that the analogy with Costanza does not apply completely and wholly to Piccarda, or that her reasoning does not account entirely for the grammar of the canto, is to say that the light of the sun does not completely cover the moon, but leaves dark spots. Piccarda is one of these dark spots.

The condemnation of Piccarda, as usual in the cantica of *Paradiso*, is done, indirectly and with humour. Besides the explanation offered in *Paradiso* IV, one can reread Piccarda's speech to pick up Dante's subtle hints about her lack of vocation. As we have already indicated, not only is she introduced as 'vaga' (34) but she also prides herself at being very beautiful, 'non mi ti celerà l'esser più bella' [it will not be hidden from you that I am most beautiful] (*Par.* III, 48), which is hardly what should be emphasized by someone who once aspired to become a nun. In her speech, we can read that she is surprised to be among these blessed souls, where, in fact, she does not belong: 'ma riconoscerai ch'i' son Piccarda,/ che, posta qui con questi altri beati,/ beata sono in la spera più tarda' [you will recognize that I am Piccarda, who was put here with these other blessed, and blessed I am in this slowest of spheres] (49–51). We are not meant to take this statement as an example of humility, but literally that Piccarda is only 'beata' by association, or by reflection. Once again the repetition of 'beati' 'beata' does not make her blessed, but points to the fact that she considers herself to be 'blessed,' figuratively; that is, fortunate to be with the other blessed in the Heaven of the Moon, where she really does not belong.

As is the case throughout the *Paradiso*, where each heaven is structured in three parts, which usually take up three cantos, in this Heaven of the Moon the first canto sets the theme, the second illustrates it by means of an allegorical narrative, and the third, the more didactic one, concludes by addressing the particular issue directly. In canto II, we have the theory of Moon spots, in canto III, an illustration of the theory through the allegorical tale of Piccarda and Costanza, and in canto IV, and part of canto V, a discussion of unfulfilled vows. In this last canto of the triad, Dante tries to answer the question why, when someone else is responsible for breaking the vows, as in Piccarda's case, this entails a diminution of the person's worthiness with respect to God: 'Se 'l buon voler dura,/ la violenza altrui per qual ragione/ di meritar mi scema la misura?' [If the right will endures, on what ground does another's violence lessen the measure of my desert?'] (*Par.* IV, 19–21). Dante also wants to know why the souls return to the stars, confirming what Plato seems to have believed. Beatrice answers the second question first because it is more dangerous, 'piú di felle' [has more poison in it] (27). The answer, given by Beatrice, essentially anticipates what Piccarda has already stated. All souls enjoy equal status and equal divine love despite how they appear to Dante, which is according to their spiritual level, 'Qui si mostraron, non perchè sortita/ sia questa spera lor, ma per far segno/della celestial c'ha men salita' [They have shown themselves here, not because this sphere is allotted to them, but as a sign of the heavenly rank that is least exalted] (*Par.* IV, 38–9). All the blessed souls are equal amongst themselves; the apparent difference exists only for Dante's sake, that is, for the sake of poetic representation. Human understanding cannot comprehend undifferentiated knowledge. Human knowledge is knowledge of difference that distinguishes between two otherwise similar entities. Without this difference, this 'far segno,' which is another way to refer to poetic language or just to language in general, understanding would be impossible. Beatrice's answer reiterates the modus operandi of the *Paradiso* and its poetic function, and insists on the necessity of personification, or allegory, in representing what in itself cannot be represented:

> Per questo la Scrittura condescende
>   a vostra facultate, e piedi e mano
>   attribuisce a Dio, ed altro intende.
>   (*Par.* IV, 43–5)

[For this reason Scripture condescends to your capacity and attributes hands and feet to God, meaning something else.]

In Beatrice's explanation, Dante is very eager to avoid any possible similarity with Plato's *Timaeus*. The poison (felle) consists, precisely, in the potential confusion between the Platonic model and the Christian one. At the same time, his answer is an example of how language changes over time, since when Plato wrote the *Timaeus* he employed words that now can no longer be deciphered. While what is stated in Plato does not correspond to what we find in the Heavens, Plato seems to believe in what he writes: 'Quel che Timeo dell'anime argomenta/ non è simile a ciò che qui si vede,/ però che, come dice, par che senta' [What Timaeus argues about the souls is not like that which we have here; for what he says he seems to hold for truth] (*Par.* IV, 49–51). While what Plato states is certainly not the case, his statement can also be read in a different way: 'e forse sua sentenza è d'altra guisa/che la voce non suona, ed esser puote/ con intenzion da non esser derisa' [but perhaps his view is other than his words express and may have a meaning not to be despised] (55–7). If he means to say that the honour and the blame of their influence is what returns, then he is not far from the truth. 'S'elli intende tornare a queste ruote/ l'onor della influenza e 'l biasmo, forse/ in alcun vero suo arco percuote' [If he means the return to these wheels of the honour and the blame of their influence, his bow perhaps hits on some truth] (58–60). Reading the *Timaeus* and interpreting what Plato meant has been the cause of much misunderstanding precisely because of the ambiguous way with which he stated it, and because language is in constant flux, and what seemed appropriate and meaningful in Plato's time is not at present.

The answer to Dante's first doubt concerns divine justice and whether violence done to interfere with the two women's vows should be held against them. Beatrice's answer is that they can be held accountable because they partake of the violence that was done to them: 'ché volontà, se non vuol, non s'ammorza/ma fa come natura face in foco,/ se mille volte violenza il torza' [for will, if it will not, is not quenched, but does as nature does in fire though violence wrench it aside a thousand times] (*Par.* IV, 76–8). These women capitulated to the will of others and did not go back to their convent, whenever the occasion arose: 'e così queste fero,/ possendo rifuggir nel santo loco' [and this they did when they might have fled back to the holy place] (80–1). Had they had unbending will, which is rare, their will would have brought them back the moment they were set free: 'così l'avria ripinte per la strada/ ond'eran tratte, come fuoro sciolte/ ma così salda voglia è troppo rada' [so [their will] would have brought them back where they were abducted, but will so firm is rare indeed] (86–7).

But Beatrice's claim seems to be contradicted by Piccarda's story that Costanza had kept her vows: 'l'affezion del vel Costanza tenne' (*Par.* IV, 98); and blessed souls do not lie – 'Ch'alma beata non poria mentire' [a blessed soul cannot lie] (95); since they share in divine truth – 'però ch'è sempre al primo vero appresso' [since it is always near the truth] (96). Beatrice's reply is another example of differentiation. She argues that sometimes, in order to avoid a major harm, man performs an even greater harm. In these cases, the will of those who suffer the violence is added to the will of those who inflict it. The sins that derive from this forced cooperation of external violence and conditioned will cannot be excused: 'la forza al voler si mischia, e fanno/ sì che scusar non si posson l'offense' [force mixes with the will and they so operate that the offences cannot be excused] (107–8). In these cases, the harm generated by the will cannot be condoned, and this is what Beatrice meant to say, while Costanza's will, which Piccarda spoke about, was a universal will, which is not allowed to be in the wrong. So there is no contradiction between what Piccarda said of Costanza and what Beatrice says now, since one was talking about absolute will and the other about relative will.

> Però, quando Piccarda quello spreme,
>   della voglia assoluta intende, e io
>   dell'altra; sí che ver diciamo insieme.
>   (*Par.* IV, 112–14)

[Piccarda, therefore, in what she says, means absolute will, and I the other, so that we both speak the truth.]

The remaining canto is a reflection on this partial, relative knowledge and the doubts that it generates. Our intellect is not appeased until our understanding is completely satisfied, until it does not acquire a truth outside of which there can be no other truth:

> Io veggio ben che già mai non si sazia
>   nostro intelletto, se 'l *ver* non lo illustra
>   di fuor dal qual nessun *vero* si spazia.
>   (*Par.* IV, 124–6; emphasis mine)

[I see well that our intellect is never satisfied unless *truth* enlightens it, beyond which no *truth* can range.]

When there is more than one truth (ver), and not just one truth (vero), as in the former case, there is ambiguity and our intellect is left wondering. This is the problem of these cantos of the Heaven of the Moon, which are only partially, and only at times, illuminated by the light of the sun, or the light of reason. The presence of a 'ver' and a 'vero' creates a situation where the mind, though at an impasse, is capable, by means of doubt, to arrive at even higher truths. This argument leads Dante to ask his next and final question as to whether one can supplement broken vows with other good actions.

The answer to this question, which continues the whole discussion on promises and the doctrine of vows, is dealt with in the first part of *Paradiso* V. Vows, Beatrice explains, are not only the result of one's free will, but also of what one sacrifices, which, in taking a vow, is free will. Since free will is God's greatest gift to man, and since man has already misused it in breaking his vows, what can he now offer in its place? However, there is the fact that in these cases the Church allows dispensations, and this would seem to be in open contradiction with the general rule just indicated. Beatrice's reply is similar to the one she gave earlier with respect to Piccarda, namely, that to the essence of vows concur two elements: one formal and one material. The latter is the object of the vow, whether one promises money, fasting, or one's life; the other is the convention, the formalization of the deal to which one commits one's own free will. The latter, being a deal one makes with God, can never be annulled, except by fulfilling it. The former, instead, can be exchanged without committing a sin. The two conditions of the exchange are that they can be made only by some religious authority, and that the exchange be greater than what was promised earlier. One exception is the vow of chastity, which cannot be bested by any other promised object.

The conclusion to the doctrine on vows takes the form of an invective that man should take their vows seriously, and not 'a ciancia' [lightly] (*Par.* V, 64), as in the case of judge Jefte, who promised to sacrifice the first thing he saw if he was victorious over the Ammonites, and the person turned out to be his daughter; or, like Agamemnon, who promised to sacrifice his daughter Iphigenia if the gods sent him favourable winds to begin his conquest of Troy. 'Siate, Cristiani, a muovervi piú gravi:/ non siate come penna ad ogni vento,/ e non crediate ch'ogni acqua vi lavi' [Be graver, Christians, in your undertakings. Be not like feathers in every wind, and think not that every water will wash you clean] (73–5).

However, Beatrice's invective against reckless vows made for personal gain, and her exhortation to read 'il novo e 'l vecchio Testamento' [the New and the Old Testaments] (*Par.* V, 76), properly and prudently, is not without irony when she suggests that people should follow the example of popes in order to reach salvation: 'e 'l pastor della Chiesa che vi guida:/questo vi basti a vostro salvamento' [and the Shepherd of the Church to guide you; let that suffice for your salvation] (77–8). Earlier, Beatrice had alluded to the corrupt state of the Church that annulled and commuted vows for its own gain: 'perché Santa Chiesa in ciò dispensa' [since Holy Church gives dispensations in this matter] (35). The Church is itself an example of that 'mala cupidigia' that Beatrice denounces:

Se mala cupidigia altro vi grida,
   uomini siate, e non pecore matte,
   sí che 'l Giudeo di voi tra voi non rida!
(*Par.* V, 79–81)

[If wicked greed tries to sway you, be men, not senseless sheep, that the Jew in your midst may not laugh at you!]

Beatrice's invective terminates the events of the Heaven of the Moon, narrated over three and a half cantos. Her constant attempts to answer Dante's doubts are an attempt to cover all angles and leave no space empty without truth: 'se 'l ver non lo illustra/di fuor dal qual nessun vero si spazia' (*Par.* IV, 125–6), which would be equivalent to the sun covering all the Moon spots. This possibility is discounted, however, when Dante confesses that he still has more questions to ask: 'mio cupido ingegno,/ che già nuove questioni avea davante' [my eager mind,/which already had new questions before it] (*Par.* V, 89–90). Doubt and truth go together. The more truth we know the more doubt is generated, and so on to infinity. One will never be able to reach a time when doubt will be completely and absolutely satisfied, or when the sun will completely cover all the moon spots. For Dante, however, it is time to move on to the Heaven of Mercury, so he puts all thoughts and all doubts aside and moves on.

2 Heaven of Mercury: Dialectics (V–VII)

E lo cielo di Mercurio si può comparare a la Dialettica per due proprietadi: che Mercurio è la più piccola stella del cielo, ché la quantitade del suo diametro non è più che di dugento trentadue miglia, secondo che pone Alfagrano, che dice quello essere de le ventotto parti una del diametro de la terra, lo quale è sei milia cinquecento miglia; *l'altra proprietade si è che più va velata de li raggi del Sole che null'altra stella.* E queste due proprietadi sono ne la Dialettica: ché la Dialettica è minore in suo corpo che null'altra scienza, ché perfattemente è compilata e terminata in quello tanto testo che ne l'Arte Vecchia e ne la Nuova si truova; *e va più velata che nulla scienza, in quanto procede con più sofistici e probabili argomenti più che altra.* (*Conv.* II, xiii, 11–12; emphasis mine)

[The heaven of Mercury may be compared to Dialectic on account of two properties, because Mercury is the smallest star in the heavens, for the length of its diameter is no more than two hundred and thirty-two miles, according to Alfraganus, who asserts that it is one twenty-eighth the diameter of the earth, which is six thousand and five hundred miles. *The second property is that it pursues its course more veiled by the rays of the sun than any other star.* These two properties are found in Dialectic, too, for Dialectic is a more compact body of knowledge than any other science, being set out in its entirety in a text no larger than the *Old Art* and the *New Art*; *it pursues its course more veiled than any other science, in that it proceeds by more subtle and hypothetical arguments than any other.*]

Halfway through canto V Dante and Beatrice move to the Heaven of Mercury, and the canto proper begins with an apostrophe to the reader:

> Pensa, lettor, se quel che qui s'inizia
> non procedesse, come tu avresti
> di piú savere angosciosa carizia;
> (*Par.* V, 109–11)

[Think, reader, if this beginning went no further how keenly you would crave to know the rest;]

The apostrophe is the first part of a comparison where Dante compares the desire of the reader if the narrative of the poem were to stop at this point, to his desire to know the people of this canto. This roundabout way to introduce the Heaven of Mercury illustrates the workings of dialectic and the way it pursues its course by subtle and hypothetical arguments.

The other purpose of the apostrophe is to provide the reader with a key to reading the three cantos that deal with the theme of justice and history. Dante alerts the reader not to trust everything he reads, since to be in the Heaven of Mercury means being exposed to sophistic and probable arguments that appear true but are not. In fact, the entire canto V insists on the importance of correct understanding, 'veggio ben' [I see well], and on not letting oneself be swayed by appearances. Beatrice explains the concept at the beginning of the canto, saying that man believes he understands, when in fact he does not. What he thinks to be the 'vero bene,' she states, is really a 'bene fallace.' The reason for this misunderstanding is a lack of discrimination between two types of good. To be sure, we are seduced by the higher good, but this exists only as a trace, a semblance of the lower good for which we settle.

> *Io veggio ben* sí come giá risplende
> nell'intelletto tuo l'etterna luce,
> che, vista, sola e sempre amore accende;
> e s'altra cosa vostro amor seduce,
> *non è se non di quella alcun vestigio,*
> *mal conosciuto, che quivi traluce.*
> (*Par.* V, 7–12; emphasis mine)

[*I see well* how there shines now in your mind the eternal light which, seen, alone and always kindles love; and if aught else beguile your love *it is nothing but some trace of this, ill-understood, that shines through there.*]

The error is to believe good what is essentially only an appearance and a trace of the higher good. This condition of the Heaven of Mercury, where sophistry and dissimulation reign supreme, is allegorized in the exchange between Dante and the main character, Justinian. The Roman Emperor first appears to Dante concealed in his light: 'Io veggio ben sì come tu t'annidi/ nel proprio lume' [I see well how you hide in your own light] (*Par.* V, 124–5). And again later,

> per più letizia *sì mi si nascose*
>   *dentro al suo raggio la figura santa;*
>   e così chiusa chiusa mi rispose
> nel mondo che 'l seguente canto canta
>   (*Par.* V, 138–9; emphasis mine)

[for more joy, *the holy form hid itself from me within its own beams* and thus all enclosed answered me in the manner the next canto sings]

We do not usually pay much attention to the words 't'annidi' and 'nascose,' and take them figuratively to mean that Justinian appeared wrapped in bright lights, for mere joy. We do not think they are meant literally that he is hiding, because we do not believe that Dante wants us to think that Justinian has anything to hide. Yet the phrase 'veggio ben' alerts the reader to the fact that appearances are misleading and that we must look well before coming to a conclusion.

Justinian's reply takes the entire canto VI and is one long, uninterrupted narrative that recounts the history of Rome, told as the history of the Eagle, up to Dante's time. This history, however, is not without problems. For one thing, Justinian's history seems to go backwards, against the dictates of heaven – 'contr'al corso del ciel' [against the course of heaven] (*Par.* VI, 2) – rather than from East to West, from the Fall of Troy to the foundation of Rome, beginning when Constantine decided to move the seat of the Roman Empire from Rome to Byzantium.

Another discrepancy is in the final reference to the Guelphs and the Ghibellines, who are said to have either misused the Eagle like the Ghibellines, or fought against it like the Guelphs:

> perché tu veggi con quanta ragione
>   si move contr'al sacrosanto segno
>   e chi 'l appropria e chi a lui s'oppone.
> (*Par.* VI, 31–3)

[so that you may see with what reason they act against the most holy standard, both those that take it for their own and those that oppose it.]

And more confusion is created from the affectionate words that Justinian has for his general, Belisarius: 'e al mio Belisar commendai l'armi' [to my Belisarius I committed arms] (*Par.* VI, 25), when, in Dante's time, it was common knowledge that Justinian had not treated him well, and had falsely accused him of plotting against him. Justinian himself adds to the bafflement when he is first introduced as 'Cesare fui e son Iustiniano') [I was Caesar and am Justinian] (*Par.* VI, 10), a declaration which has always been interpreted as an example of his newly found humility, now that he is in Paradise, where he is no longer a Roman emperor but just another man.

Within the context of the Heaven of Mercury and dialectic, these contradictory statements should be taken as so many instances of sophistry, as a way of hiding a not too pleasant past. One reason to hide is Justinian's belief, which he shared with the monotheists of his time, that Christ possessed only one nature: 'una natura in Cristo esser (...) credea, e di tal fede era contento;' [I believed [...] Christ to have one nature and I was satisfied with that belief] (*Par.* VI, 14–15). We know that Pope Agapitus persuaded him to the contrary, and that he eventually believed in the two natures of Christ. However, it appears that only in Paradise he found confirmation of what the Pope told him:

Io li credetti; e ciò che 'n sua fede era,
vegg'io or chiaro sí, come tu vedi
ogni contradizione e falsa e vera.
(*Par.* VI, 19–21; emphasis mine)

[I believed him, and what he held by faith *I now see as clearly as you see that every contradiction is both true and false.*]

However, the clarity that Justinian seems to have acquired in heaven is suspect when it is compared to a contradiction that is both true and false. The implication is that Justinian still believes that a dual nature in Christ is a contradiction.

For all these reasons, Justinian's entire speech on the progress of the history of the Eagle, starting with 'Vedi quanta virtú l'ha fatto degno/di reverenza' [See what virtue made it worthy of reverence] (*Par.* VI, 34–5), can and should be read ironically. The line, in fact, implies the opposite of what it states. Rather than proving the political and military virtue which made the Eagle worthy of being revered, it wants to state that this virtue was very much lacking.

The history of the Eagle's 'virtue' begins, fittingly, where Virgil's *Aeneid* left off, and, more specifically, with the death of Pallas: 'Vedi quanta virtù l'ha fatto degno/ di riverenza; e cominciò dall'ora/ che Pallante morí per darli regno' [See what virtue made it worthy of reverence, beginning from the hour when Pallas died to give it sway] (*Par.* VI, 35–6). To all appearances this is a welcome event because it coincides with Aeneas' 'just' killing of Turnus, which ushers in a new era of prosperity for Italy, and leads, eventually, to the foundation of Rome. Yet, as I have indicated in my analysis of *Inferno* II and of Virgil's prophecy in *Reading Dante Reading*, the death of Pallas implies rather the opposite, an injustice. Aeneas' killing of Turnus in just vengeance for the death of Pallas is really an excuse to be rid of his rival once and for all. Turnus' protestations at this injustice, 'The unconsenting spirit fled to the shades below' (*Aeneid* XII, 952), voice Virgil's objections at this useless and senseless killing, one more instance of Roman injustice. Dante's choice to begin the history of the Eagle from an injustice is his way of undercutting both Justinian and the history of the Eagle as the history of justice. The history of the Eagle is in fact a history of oppressions, kidnappings (the Sabine women), unscrupulous tyrants (Tarquinus the arrogant), and violence. With the story of Julius Caesar (*Par.* VI, 55–72) we begin the account of Rome's civil wars, the darkest period in Roman history, which Dante lifts straight out of Lucan's *Pharsalia,* the epic that the Roman author wrote to condemn Caesar and all his descendents. (See chap. 5 for further discussion on this point.)

But the rhetoric of this canto, with its contrived argumentation, is most clear in examples of justice similar to that of Aeneas' killing of Turnus in just vengeance for the death of Pallas. The first example of just punishment is the crucifixion of Christ under the Emperor Tiberius. This 'justice,' which to all appearance is inscrutable, 'in apparenza poco e scuro' [in appearance somewhat obscure] (*Par.* VI, 85), regards the killing of Christ as just retribution for Adam's sin:

ché la viva giustizia che mi spira,
  li concedette, in mano a quel ch'io dico,
  gloria di far vendetta alla sua ira.
(*Par.* VI, 88–90)

[for the living justice that inspires me, granted it, in the hand of whom I speak, the glory of doing vengeance for his wrath.]

The spuriousness of Justinian's argument is made clear in the passage where he tries to justify the destruction of Jerusalem as punishment for having crucified Christ: 'poscia con Tito a far vendetta corse/ della vendetta del peccato antico' [afterwards it ran with Tito to do vengeance on the vengeance for the ancient sin] (*Par.* VI, 92–3). Just as Aeneas's killing of Turnus is really an excuse to be rid of his rival, Justinian justifies titus' senseless destruction of Jerusalem as an act of vengeance for the killing of Christ, when he had previously justified the same killing of Christ under Tiberius because of Adam's sin!

The final invective against the Guelphs and Ghibellines, as I indicated, concerns their false operating under the sign of the Eagle, each for their own devious designs: the Guelphs who oppose it by siding with the golden lilies of the Anjou of the House of France; and the Ghibellines who appropriate the symbol of the Eagle to perpetrate their own crimes. The Guelphs and Ghibellines perpetuate the deception of Aeneas and Justinian, who, under the sign of the Eagle and of Justice, perpetrate their murderous crimes as acts of justice.

The latter part of *Paradiso* VI is taken up with an explanation of the souls that appear in the Heaven of Mercury, which is a further example of Justinian's spurious argumentation. Here we find the souls of the ambitious and avid of earthly glory who find themselves in this heaven because they have fallen short in their love of God.

> Questa picciola stella si correda
> di buoni spirti che son stati attivi
> perché onore e fama li succeda:
> e quando li disiri poggian quivi,
> sì disviando, pur convien che i raggi
> del vero amore in su poggian men vivi.
> (*Par.* VI, 112–17)

[This little star is adorned with good spirits whose deeds were done for the honour and glory that should follow them; and when desires mount here, thus deviating them, the rays of true love must needs mount upwards with less life.]

These souls are not chastised for having been ambitious (*attivi*) or for having sought honour and fame, but because their desires were motivated by personal ambition (poggian quivi) and not by love of Justice and love of God. They came up short and now appear in the Heaven of Mercury.

Amongst these, ironically, is the example of Romée de Villeneuve, last mentioned by Justinian, who is similarly an example of injustice: 'di cui/fu l'ovra grande e bella mal gradita' [whose great and noble work was ill rewarded] (*Par.* VI, 128–9). As Sapegno points out, Dante seems to accept the legend that Romée, coming back from a pilgrimage and having heard that Count Raimondo Berengario of Provence was a good man, decided to stay at his court, where he not only proved to be a wise counsellor, tripling the Count's income, but he also gave him good advice so that the Count could marry his four daughters honourably. But the envy of those at court turned the Count against Romée, accusing him of having poorly administered his wealth. Romée in reply told the Count that during his stay he had lived honestly, with only the Count's well-being and interest in mind. But now that the Count, influenced by false counsellors, was showing little gratitude, he wished to leave with the little he had when he arrived. The Count did not want him to go, but Romée left as he had come, and no one saw him ever again.

The example of Romée, 'persona umile e peregrina' [a person of low birth and a stranger] (*Par.* VI, 135), is important on many levels. He is an example of how one can easily misjudge others, especially those who act in all honesty and goodwill, and who easily become the object of the envy of others. The reason, however, that we find the story of Romée in Justinian's speech is that it is a perfect parallel to the story of Justinian and his General Belisar. Commentators thought that Dante did not know the story of Justinian's mistreatment of his faithful general, swayed by the false accusations of his envious accusers. But Dante did, and the story of Romée is proof, because the only reason to include it in this canto, the Heaven of Mercury, as an example of injustice, is to indirectly reflect on Justinian's injustice at the expense of his loyal general. The example of Romée is a way of punishing Justinian, indirectly, for his arrogance, lack of gratitude, and injustice – a good reason, in other words, for Justinian to want to separate himself from the emperor he was and the man he is in the Heaven of Mercury. The separation, 'Cesare fui e son Iustiniano' [I was Caesar and am Justinian] (10), rather than a sign of humility, is a sign of the division inherent in characters like Justinian and Aeneas, who appear just and God-fearing but are really only intent on furthering their ambition and glory.

The Heaven of Mercury is also divided into three cantos: the first presents the main issue, the second illustrates it, and the third concludes it with a general condemnation of the flaw or the sin. In *Paradiso* VII, the apparent contradictions raised in the previous two cantos appear to find a resolution. Once again, Dante's doubts bring about the first question: How just is just vengeance? and 'come giusta vendetta giustamente/punita fosse' [how just vengeance should be justly avenged] (*Par.* VII, 20–1). The reference is once again to the destruction of Jerusalem as punishment for the death of Christ. As in Heaven of the Moon, the answer does not contradict what was said before, or, as in this case, absolve Titus from the suspicion that he destroyed Jerusalem to assert his own power and rule. The answer provided by Beatrice brings up the issue of Christ's dual nature. Christ's death is justified when Christ is understood as God who became man to redeem mankind of the sin incurred by Adam. But when Christ is understood as a man who perished as the result of the Jews' hatred, His death is not justified. In the first case, His death was a high example of justice, and infinite mercy, but with respect to the Jews who ordered it, it was a great sin, so much so that the entire earth trembled:

> Però d'un atto uscir cose diverse:
>   ch'a Dio ed a' Giudei piacque una morte;
>   per lei tremò la terra e 'l ciel s'aperse.
> (*Par.* VII, 46–8)

[From one act, therefore, came diverse effects, for the same death was pleasing both to God and to the Jews; because of it earth quaked and heaven opened.]

According to Beatrice and her reasoning, the destruction of Jerusalem was more than justified: 'giusta vendetta/poscia vengiata fu da giusta corte' [just vengeance was afterwards avenged by a just court] (*Par.* VII, 50–1). The reasoning, however, is not without irony, since the argument is predicated on the belief in Christ's dual nature. If one believes in Christ as having only a divine nature, as Justinian did, then His dying on the Cross is sufficient to mankind's redemption, and the destruction of Jerusalem is simply an act of brutality and personal ambition. If one believes in both the divine and the human nature of Christ, the destruction of Jerusalem is justified and there is just vengeance. According to this spurious argument, it would behoove Justinian to believe in

Christ's double nature. It is perhaps for this reason that once in heaven, Dante leaves him with no choice but to accept it.

As in the Heaven of the Moon, once a doubt is resolved it only generates more doubt. Now Dante wants to know why God chose the incarnation and passion of Christ to redeem mankind. At this point it is clear that Dante wants to add his views to the age-old question of reincarnation, on which much has been said and written: 'molto si mira e poco si discerne' [much has been aimed at this mark and little discernment] (*Par.* VII, 62). According to Dante's doctrine of redemption, there are only two ways in which God could have avenged Adam's transgression. He could have either condoned his sin, or he could have let man remedy his folly, by his powers alone. While the former was not possible, the second was even more impossible given that man, a finite being, could never adequately satisfy divine justice. 'Non potea l'uomo ne' termini suoi/ mai sodisfar, per non potere ir giuso/ con umiltate obediendo poi, quando disobediendo intese ir suso' [Man could never, within his limits, give satisfaction, for he could not go so low in humility, by a later obedience, as, by disobedience, he had to go high] (96–9). God's way was to use both solutions: to help man by empowering him with Christ as a man-god. While man's humiliation would not have sufficed to make up for Adam's sin, the reincarnation of the Son of God could.

At this point, Beatrice introduces a corollary, as she does elsewhere in similar circumstances, so that the perspective of Dante the pilgrim can be adjusted to her own: 'perché tu veggi lí cosí com'io' [so you may see it as clearly as I do] (*Par.* VII, 123). Since Beatrice had stated that whatever was created directly by God is immortal, Dante asks why the four elements are not free from corruption: 'da corruzion sicure' [they should be secure from corruption] (129). According to Beatrice, only the angels and the heavens can be said to be created directly by God, whereas the elements are just creations, 'da creata virtù' [by created virtue] (135). The intellectual soul is also directly created by God, whose absolute goodness the soul desires, so that it absolutely desires to return to God. This is proof, says Beatrice, not only of the immortality of the soul, but also that at the end of the world, our bodies will be resurrected and will rejoin their souls. The final corollary reiterates the duality of body and soul, which ensures immortality to mankind but in which Justinian did not believe.

The Heaven of Mercury, in its affiliation with dialectic, exposes the sophistry behind Justinian's history of the Eagle as the history of Justice, revealing the deception and the corruption concealed behind claims of virtue and justice. As in the previous Heaven of the Moon, the deception is denounced and punished, indirectly, by reflection or by analogy, through parallel examples. In this manner Dante fulfils his role as DXV to provide a critique of Empire and Emperors whose ambition and desire for worldly glory has made them betray their divine mandate, to serve mankind and the greater glory of God.

3 Heaven of Venus: Rhetoric (VIII–IX)

E lo cielo di Venere si può comparare a la Rettorica per due propietadi: l'una sí è la chiarezza del suo aspetto, che è soavissima a vedere piú che altra stella; l'altra si è la sua apparenza, or da mane or da sera. E queste due proprietadi sono ne la Rettorica: ché la Rettorica è soavissima di tutte le altre scienze, però che a ciò principalmente intende; e appare da mane, quando dinanzi al viso de l'uditore lo rettorico parla, appare da sera, cioè retro, quando da la terra, per la parte remota, si parla per lo rettorico.[1] (*Conv.* II, xiii, 13–14)

[The heaven of Venus may be compared to Rhetoric on account of two properties: the first is the clarity of its appearance, which is sweeter to behold than that of any other star; the second is its appearance in the morning and in the evening. These two properties are in Rhetoric, which is the sweetest of all the other sciences, and it appears in the morning when the rhetorician speaks directly before an audience, and in the evening, that is, from behind, when the rhetorician speaks from the earth, from the remote side.]

At the beginning of *Paradiso* VIII, and alluding to the Heaven of Venus in which he now finds himself, Dante differentiates this heaven

---

1 The Busnelli-Vandelli edition reads 'lettera' instead of 'la terra' because, in their view, the latter does not make sense ('è una lezione che non dà senso'). They forget that the Heaven of Venus shares properties with the earth and that the hidden part (da retro) is precisely the part that comes from the earth, 'la terra.' *Il Convivio, ridotto a miglior lezione e commentats da G. Busnelli e G. Vandelli, con introduzione di Michele Barbi* (Florence: Le Monnier, 1934–37).

from the ancient notion of Venus the goddess of 'mad love' (folle amore) (*Par.* VIII, 2), and refers to this ancient belief as error: 'le genti antiche nell'antico errore' [the ancient peoples in their ancient error] (5). The reference to 'folle amor' is to Virgil's *Aeneid* and to Dido, and more explicitly to Venus' fears that her son Aeneas may not be welcome at her court because of Juno's constant interference with her son's voyage. Venus instructs her other son Cupid to take the place of Aeneas' son Ascanius and to light in Dido the flame of love for Aeneas. The reference to 'folle amore' is to Dido's madness when Aeneas leaves her to continue his journey to Italy. The example characterizes the dual aspect of Venus and love: good love, which is that of a mother worried for her son's safety; and 'folle amore,' the love born of passion and that is unrequited. They are the positive and negative faces of Venus with respect to the sun, when she appears behind it as Hesperus, and in front as Lucipher.

> e da costei ond'io principio piglio
>   pigliavano il vocabol della stella
>   che 'l sol vagheggia or da coppa, or da ciglio.
> (*Par.* VIII, 10–12)

[and from her from whom I take my start they took the name of the star that woos the sun, now from behind, now in front.]

This dual aspect of love, as the morning and evening sides of Venus, its apparent and hidden aspects ('da mane' and 'retro'), respectively, parallels the duality of rhetoric, to which the Heaven of Venus corresponds: its overt aspect that appeals to an audience as persuasion and its hidden aspect as trope, which is the rhetorical and unpredictable side of language. But these two aspects are not really separate from one another. Just as good love is inherently related to mad love, and are in appearance both virtuous and in error, so good and bad rhetoric, or rhetoric as persuasion and rhetoric as trope, are always inextricably present and interwoven with one another.

This dual aspect of Venus has implications for the other two heavens with which it is grouped, Moon and Mercury, as all three partake of both earthly and heavenly elements. This implies that rhetoric also affects the functioning of Grammar and Dialectic, positively or negatively, as the case may be, with which it is related as one of the three Liberal Arts of the *Trivium*. This relation of identity and difference is exemplified in the souls Dante encounters in these cantos, who like to exhibit their heavenly side and try to hide their earthly one, to make their virtue manifest while trying to hide their 'ancient' errors. The task of the reader is to read the dissimulation concealed in the rhetoric of these souls, which is revealed through irony, in an effort to bring about Dante's critique of Empire and of the corrupt history of the Eagle.

The first soul Dante meets in this canto is Charles Martel, who, in speaking for the rest of the souls in this sphere, welcomes Dante by declaring that they are full of love for him: 'e sem sí pien d'amor [we are so full of love] (*Par.* VIII, 38). Charles Martel's enthusiasm, surprising as it has always appeared to readers, is suspect from the start because of its association with love as pleasure:

> e solo incominciò: 'Tutti sem presti
> al tuo *piacer*, perché di noi ti gioi.
> (*Par.* VIII, 32–3; emphasis mine)

> [and began alone: 'We are all ready at your *pleasure* so that you may have joy of us.]

The emphasis on 'amor' is understandable in Paradise and in this heaven, but the mention of 'piacer' is questionable, since whenever it is a question of 'piacer,' it is also a question of the earthly type of love that leads to 'folle amore.'

Charles Martel quotes the first line of the first *canzone* which Dante cites in the *Convivio*: 'Voi che 'ntendendo il terzo ciel movete' [You who by understanding move the third heaven], which, besides referring to Venus, the third heaven (terzo ciel), also alludes to Dante's love for philosophy. As we know, the *canzone* is the poet's confession to the souls that move the Heaven of Venus of his new love: 'Io vi dirò del cor la novitate' [I shall speak to you of the novel condition of my heart] (*Canzone* I, 10). The episode recalls *Purgatory* II and Dante's meeting with Casella, where it is also a question of a *canzone* in praise of philosophy: 'Amor che ne la mente mi ragiona' [Love which discourses in my mind] (*Purg.* II, 112), which the souls appreciate for the pleasure it provides rather than for its edifying philosophical meaning. Charles Martel, likewise, quotes the *canzone* not for its philosophical implications but for the pleasure and the love with which the song fills him. Charles is a reader of the *canzone*, not of the *Convivio*, and, as the repeated reference to 'piacer' and to 'dolce' indicates, he is a literal reader who takes the *canzone* to be celebrating the pleasures of love and not the allegorical love for the 'donna gentile' and philosophy.

> e *sem sí pien d'amor*, che, per *piacerti*,
> non fia men *dolce* un poco di quiete.'
> (*Par.* VIII, 389–9; emphasis mine)

[and *we are so full of love* that, in order to *please you*, a little quiet will not be less *sweet*.']

Charles Martel, we could say, is like one of those readers who misread Dante's *canzoni*, making it necessary for him to write the *Convivio* and explain them. But Dante does not reproach him. After all, what could one expect from a future emperor who died at the age of twenty-four?

Dante's reaction to Charles' welcome is a glance at Beatrice that reveals the irony of the passage, since Dante's 'donna' is the 'donna gentile,' not Beatrice, who, as the figure of poetry, is only the poetic representation that mediates the philosophical doctrine: 'Poscia che li occhi miei si fuoro offerti/alla mia donna reverenti' [After my eyes had been raised with reverence to my Lady] (*Par.* VIII, 40–1). As I indicated in my reading of *Inferno* II, Dante condemns the love poetry of the *Vita nuova*, written for Beatrice, as well as the poetry of his predecessors and contemporaries that in modern times, ironically, has come to be known as the school of the 'dolce stil nuovo' [sweet new style], because from its Provençal origins to Guido Guinizelli it exemplifies a type of poetry inspired by love as pleasure, rather than love of knowledge, wisdom, and virtue.

Charles Martel's reaction to Dante's *canzone* reveals most of all his immaturity and lack of wisdom and virtue. When Charles Martel first appears, he is described as veiled and wrapped in his joy (letizia). The image seems positive at first, but on closer analysis it compares Charles to a silkworm that has not fully developed into a butterfly. This shortcoming is one of the reasons why his identity is kept hidden, concealed by his 'letizia':

> La mia letizia mi tien celato
>   che mi raggia dintorno e mi nasconde
>   quasi animal di sua seta fasciato.
> (*Par.* VIII, 52–4)

[My happiness which shines around me hides me from you and conceals me like a creature swathed in its own silk.]

Charles Martel is never introduced or mentioned by name but he is identified, indirectly, through the love that Dante, supposedly, had for him: 'Assai m'amasti' [You loved me much] (*Par.* VIII, 55). Critics, for example C.H. Grandgent, have inferred that Charles Martel must have met Dante during his visit to Florence in 1294, or that he admired Dante's 'perfect calligraphy' and certainly his *canzone*, which he quotes in this canto, and 'which was *presumably* the great literary novelty in Florence at the time of his visit.'[2] This is pure speculation on Grandgent's part, and there is no reason to believe that any of it is true. Certainly, if Charles quotes the *canzone* in the canto it is not because he remembers it but because Dante, in creating the episode, makes him say that. The reasons are not obvious at first, but, as I have indicated, the reference to the *canzone* and to love as 'piacere' serve to indicate that Charles and the other souls in this heaven are still at an early stage of their spiritual development, the stage of love as pleasure, and they have not yet learned the true value of love, the love of Lady Philosophy, the love of wisdom and virtue that Dante, at the beginning of the poem, speaks of as the nourishment that the Veltro, or his *Commedia,* will provide for its readers.

The reasons why Charles says what he does and why it is stated indirectly, are deeper and well disguised. The canto, in fact, develops on the basis of a series of hypotheses, foremost amongst them Dante's love for him, which is undocumented, as his promise that if he had lived longer he would have shown his true affection for the poet.

> Assai m'amasti, e avesti ben onde;
>   ché s'io fossi giú stato, io ti mostrava
>   di mio amor piú oltre che le fronde.
>   (*Par.* VIII, 55–7)

[You loved me much, and had good cause; for had I been below I would have shown you much more of my love than leaves.]

---

2 From *La Divina Commedia of Dante Alighieri*, edited and annotated by C.H. Grandgent. Revised by Charles Singleton (Cambridge, MA: Harvard University Press, 1972), 692.

Even more important is the claim that if he had not died young, at age twenty-four, he would have been a great ruler and a lot of evil would have been avoided.

> Così fatta, mi disse: 'Il mondo m'ebbe
> giú poco tempo; e se piú fosse stato
> molto sarà di mal, che non sarebbe.
> (*Par.* VIII, 49–51)

[So changed, it said to me: 'The world held me but a short time below, and had it been longer much evil that will be would not have been.]

Although Charles' claims have always gone unquestioned, are we to believe that this was what Dante believed? There are reasons to believe that this is not the case, not the least of which is the claim that Dante's love is unfounded, but also because it is based on speculation about what could have been. In fact, his claim is rhetorical and hides more than it reveals.

According to the modalities of the Heavens of Venus and of rhetoric, Charles speaks definitively not with 'chiarezza' but by 'apparenza,' that is, indirectly, from behind 'dosso' (*Par.* VIII, 96). This is the expression used by Charles to explain how it is possible that a good plant can produce a bad fruit: 'com'esser può di dolce seme, amaro' [how can from sweet seed come bitter] (93).

> Questo io a lui; ed elli a me: 'S'io posso
> mostrarti un vero, a quel che tu dimandi
> terrà' il viso *come tieni 'l dosso.*'
> (*Par.* VIII, 94–6; emphasis mine)

[I spoke to him so, and he replied: 'If I can show thee one truth, you will then have before your eyes the answer to your question which is *now behind your back.*']

Charles is saying that after his explanation everything will be clear to Dante, and what is now hidden, or behind him, will be clear and in front of him. With this rhetorical manoeuvre, Dante means to turn Charles right around and bring to light what Charles has been hiding all along: his lineage – that he is Charles Martel, the son of Charles II of Anjou of the House of France.

Dante's critique of the infamous House of France, which in the apocalyptic vision at the end of *Purgatory* is symbolized by the giant that revels with the harlot (the Church) and receives in this Heaven of Venus its well-deserved punishment. Indirectly, Charles Martel criticizes the tyrannical regime of Charles I of Anjou against whom the people of Palermo rebelled during the Sicilian Vespers, throwing out the French and replacing them with Peter III of Aragon (*Par.* VIII, 67–70). Charles regrets that Sicily fell in the hands of the Aragonese, and is very critical of the Angevins' misrule: 'se mala signoria, che sempre accora/li popoli suggetti, non avesse/mosso Palermo a gridar: 'Mora, mora!' [if bad rule, which always exasperates subject people, had not moved Palermo to cry 'Death, death to them!'] (73–5). Charles is equally critical of the rule of his brother Robert of Anjou, King of Naples, whose stingy nature, bad government, and misguided association with the Catalans, which he protects, risks stirring his own people against him (58–63).

Dante's indirect critique of the House of France, through Charles Martel, also takes the form of a doubt concerning how it can be possible that Charles I and Robert of Anjou are the offspring of liberal and exceptional ancestors. 'La sua natura, che di larga parca/ discese' [His mean nature descended from a generous one] (*Par.* VIII, 82–3). Commentators, understandably, have had difficulty with this passage because they could not find very liberal leaders in Charles' ancestry. In fact, as Sapegno points out, his father, Charles II, was himself a miser who Dante condemns in *Purgatory* XX (79–84), and repeatedly throughout the *Commedia*: 'Checché se ne dica, la *natura larga* non può essere quella del padre Carlo II, bollato proprio per un gesto d'avarizia in *Purgatory* XX') [Whatever one may say, the generous nature cannot be that of Charles II, who is accused precisely of avarice in *Purgatory* XX]. Sapegno finally finds amongst Robert's ancestry Charles I, who had the fame of being a liberal, and who Dante does not judge too harshly, 'esprime un giudizio meno severo' [expresses a less severe judgment]. However, the whole episode is meant ironically because Dante wants to show, on the contrary, that Robert of Anjou was indeed the son of Charles II, whose avarice was passed from the father directly to the son. But the irony is meant primarily for Charles Martel, who has criticized his brother Robert for being a miser. If the father and brother were misers, how could Charles Martel not be affected by the same malady?

Charles Martel's explanation is that human nature is such that a son would follow the inclinations of the father if it were not for the intervention of Divine Providence:

Natura generata il suo cammino
  simil farebbe sempre a' generati,
  se non vincesse il proveder divino.
(*Par.* VIII, 133–5)

[The begotten nature would always take a like course with its begetters if Divine Providence did not overrule.]

Charles mentions the example of Esau and Jacob, who, even though twin brothers, were clearly very different from one another: 'Quinci addivien ch'Esaú si diparte/per seme da Iacòb' [whence it happens that Esau differs in the seed from Jacob] (*Par.* VIII, 130–1). Similarly, Quirinus (Romulus), who comes from a very humble father, by divine intervention, is said to have been generated by Mars: 'e vien Quirino/ da sí vil padre, che si rende a Marte' [and Quirinus comes from so base a father that he is ascribed to Mars] (131–2). According to these examples, the possibility exists for Charles Martel, who died at an early age, to turn out differently from his father and from his brothers, Charles I and Robert of Anjou. However, Dante adds another corollary to this rule. Charles also posits the possibility that *fortuna* may intervene to undermine these plans, when, for instance, the natural disposition of a person is discordant with the external conditions in which he finds himself; in which case, the results are disastrous:

Sempre natura, se fortuna trova
  discorde a sé, com'ogni altra semente
  fuor di sua region, fa mala prova.
(*Par.* VIII, 139–41)

[Always, if nature meets with fortune unsuited to it, like any kind of seed out of its own region, it has ill success.]

If circumstances are discordant with the natural disposition of the person nothing good will come of it. Once again, the critique is directed at Charles Martel's brothers. Louis of Anjou, who became a friar, could probably have been a better king, whereas Robert, who was very religious and a bad king, would have made a better friar.

Ma voi torcete alla religione
  tal che fia nato a cignersi la spada,
  e fate re di tal ch'è da sermone:

Onde la traccia vostra è fuor di strada.'
  (*Par.* VIII, 145–8)

[But you wrest to religion one born to gird on the sword, and you make a king of one that is fit for sermons: so that your track is off the road.']

In the last instance, man always acts according to his own volition despite what Divine Providence has planned for him. This conclusion eliminates any possibility that Charles Martel could have turned out to be a better king than his brothers, even with the help of Divine Providence. But we have also a sense that Providence has intervened in Charles Martel's case, ironically, to save him from having to suffer a similar fate as his brothers, by making him die young and placing him in Paradise among the blessed souls. This probably explains why Charles Martel, again ironically, believes that Dante loved him very much: 'Assai m'amasti' (*Par.* VIII, 55).

Paradiso IX begins with a prediction that Charles Martel left Dante of the future evils that will visit the Angevin dynasty, but about which he has to remain silent:

> mi narrò li 'nganni
> che ricever dovea la sua semenza;
> ma disse: 'Taci, e lascia volger li anni;
> sí ch'io non posso dir se non che pianto
> giusto verrà di retro ai vostri danni.
>   (*Par.* IX, 2–6)

[he told me of the treacheries his seed was to suffer, but said: 'Be silent, and let the years revolve'; so that I can say nothing but that deserved sorrows shall follow on your wrongs.]

Commentators believe that Dante wants to allude to the plot that deprived Charles Martel's son, Charles Robert, of the Kingdom of Naples, a plot orchestrated by his uncle Robert with the support of Pope Clement V. But, once again, what Dante is mainly referring to is the action of the DXV, which has, in fact, come to expose and denounce the ills of the House of France. Dante concludes with a further invective against the Angevins and the vanity of all human desire:

> Ahi anime ingannate e fatture empie,
> che da sí fatto ben torcete i cori,

drizzando in vanità le vostre tempie!
(*Par.* IX, 10-12)

[Ah, souls beguiled, creatures without reverence, who from the good you turn away your hearts, directing your brows to vanity!]

The purpose of the remaining *Paradiso* IX is to elaborate on the theme of Providence that Charles Martel introduced in the previous canto. Cunizza da Romano's story illustrates the workings of Divine Providence, which intervenes so that two brothers, in this case brother and sister, can be different in every way. Cunizza, who is born of the same parents as Ezzelino III, a very cruel tyrant who now lies in a sea of blood in *Inferno* XII (110), is quite different from her brother. However, Cunizza was not a saint either. She was not a cruel tyrant, but she led a life of dissolution and had as many husbands as lovers, until, in her old age, she seems to have done a good deed by freeing some of her slaves. Her life is a perfect example of 'folle amore,' and she would be a good candidate for the fate of the lustful of *Inferno* V, had it not been for the intervention of Dante's Providence, which arbitrarily places her in *Paradiso* IX.

The example of Cunizza ties in with the theme of Venus stated at the beginning of canto VIII. Cunizza says that she shines in the Heaven of Venus (qui refulgo) because she was overcome by the light of this planet: 'perché mi vinse il lume d'esta stella' [because the light of this star overcame me] (*Par.* IX, 33). The influence of Venus shaped her, both when she was overcome by 'folle amore' and now, when she shines in Paradise with good love, the love of charity.

Cunizza introduces next Folquet de Marselha, ironically, as a man of great fame: 'Di questa luculenta e cara gioia/del nostro cielo che piú m'è propinqua,/ grande fama rimase' [Of this brilliant and precious jewel of our heaven that is beside me great fame was left] (*Par.* IX, 37-9). In many ways Folquet's story is similar to Cunizza's. He lived a dissolute life as a troubadour, but then repented of his previous life and became a religious man, eventually becoming a bishop. His speech begins with a geographical description similar to Cunizza's. The long periphrasis that finally alludes to Folquet's birthplace, Marseille, is also a reference to the blood of its citizens that reddened the harbour of that city. The reference is to the massacre ordered by Brutus on Caesar's orders (see *Purg.* XVIII, 102), but it also has implications for Folquet himself, implications which at first are not clear.

Folquet introduces himself as someone who belongs to the Heaven of Venus, 'e questo cielo/di me s'imprenta, com'io fe' di lui;' [and this heaven bears the stamp of me as I did of it] (*Par.* IX, 95–6), and claims that his love was no less passionate than that of Dido, Rhodope, or Hercules, who killed themselves for love. He, however, did not kill himself for love. He was a minor troubadour who celebrated with great passion Azalais, the wife of Barral du Baux, viscount of Marseille. At her death, he withdrew from the world and entered the Cistercian Order, where he became abbot of the Monastery of Torronet and later was made bishop of Toulouse. It is in this capacity that he also became a passionate and ruthless persecutor of the heretical Albigenses. The earlier reference to Brutus' bloody massacre in Marseille's harbour is meant to reflect indirectly on Folquet's own bloody massacre of the Albigenses. This is the 'grande fama' to which Cunizza alludes, ironically, and which Folquet plays down by saying that he has forgotten his guilt: 'non della colpa, ch'a mente non torna' [not for our fault, which does not come back to mind] (*Par.* IX, 104). In the Heaven of Venus, as he points out, one does not repent, one smiles: 'Non però qui si pente, ma si ride' [Here we do not repent, we smile] (103). Folquet's extreme religious zeal is not punished in Hell, but his infamous fame is sufficiently undercut by Dante's irony to make it possible to smile at Folquet's vain attempt to hide his guilt. This is the virtue of the Heaven of Venus, which turns punishment into an ironic smile: 'Si ride [...] del valor ch' ordinò e provide' [we smile [...] for the Power which ordained and foresaw] (103–5).

As Charles Martel introduces Cunizza, and Cunizza Folquet, Folquet introduces Rahab. In all these cases the introduction serves the purpose of undercutting the person introduced, who tries to conceal his or her guilt. The last figure is Rahab, the harlot who sheltered the Israelite spies making possible the destruction of the city of Jericho. Rahab, however, does not speak. She is another instance of Providence's intervention, which saves her from her fate because of a good deed. As Joshua promised her, not only was she spared when Jericho was destroyed, but she was also saved from Hell by Christ, and placed in this heaven: 'Da questo cielo ... pria ch'altr'alma/del triunfo di Cristo fu assunta' [by this heaven [...] she was taken up before any other soul of Christ's triumph] (*Par.* IX, 118–20).

The Providence that is responsible for the 'salvation' of Charles Martel, Cunizza, Folquet, and Rahab has really nothing to do with Divine Providence. Its proper name is 'Rhetoric,' the corresponding art of the Heaven of Venus, which is responsible for arbitrarily dubbing an example of 'folle amor' as good love and moving it from behind, where it was hiding, to the front, to the light of day, 'da retro a mane.' The process is as arbitrary as it is nonsensical, and it disrupts any possible expectation that we could have from following the logic, and grammar, of the argument. This is Dante's playful way to surprise his readers and foil their expectations. As Folquet points out, in the Heaven of Venus there is no punishment or penance; this is neither Hell nor Purgatory, there is only rhetoric, only irony; and the irony, this time, is also on the reader, in the form of a smile: 'Non però qui si pente, ma si ride.'

Yet the canto does not end with a smile, but with a condemnation of the city of Florence and still another prophecy. As commentators have pointed out, in this invective against Florence we get a sense of Folquet's passionate and ferocious side that he showed against the Albigenses. The city of Florence is described as Lucifer's plant, from which envy produces the cursed Florin, 'il maledetto fiore' [the accursed flower] (*Par.* IX, 130), and from where greed spreads throughout the world. The indirect reference is to *Inferno* I and to the she-wolf, the symbol of greed, of which it was said that envy generated it in Hell: 'ne lo inferno,/ là onde 'nvidia prima dipartilla' [in Hell from where envy first sent it [into the world]] (*Inf.* I, 110–11).

This final reference to greed serves to introduce the argument of the next canto, which is to denounce the greed of popes and religious leaders who are more interested in accumulating wealth than attending to their duties as spiritual leaders.

> Ma Vaticano e l'altre parti elette
> di Roma che son state cimitero
> a la milizia che Pietro seguette,
> *tosto libere fien de l'avoltero.*
> (*Par.* IX, 139–42; emphasis mine)

[But the Vatican and the other chosen parts of Rome which were the burial place of the soldiery that followed Peter will *soon be freed from that adultery*.]

The prophecy restates the mandate of the DXV to punish the Church, the adulterous harlot that consorts with the House of France. With the critique of the House of Anjou in this Heaven of Venus, the first phase of the DXV's punitive mission – to vanquish the giant and denounce the corrupt Angevin rulers – is complete. Now it is the turn of the Church, its popes, and all other religious orders that followed St Peter, 'la milizia che Pietro seguette,' which have polluted the Church from its very foundation.

This is the theme of the next cantos, beginning with the Heaven of the Sun, where the DXV turns its punitive and liberating action on the Dominican and Franciscan Orders.

4 Heaven of the Sun: Arithmetic (X–XIV)

E lo cielo del Sole si può comparare a l'Arismetrica per due proprietadi: *l'una si è che del suo lume tutte l'altre stelle s'informano; l'altra si è che l'occhio nol può mirare.* E queste due proprietadi sono ne l'Arismetrica: ché del suo lume tutte s'illuminano le scienze, però che li loro subietti sono tutti sotto alcuno numero considerati, e ne le considerazioni di quelli sempre con numero si procede. Sì come ne la scienza naturale è subietto lo corpo mobile, lo quale corpo mobile ha in sé ragione di continuitade, e questa ha in sé ragione di numero infinito; e la sua considerazione principalissima è considerare li principii de le cose naturali, li quali sono tre – cioè materia, privazione e forma – ne li quali si vede questo numero. Non solamente in tutti insieme, ma ancora in ciascuno è numero, chi ben considera sottilmente; per che Pittagora, secondo che dice Aristotile nel primo de la Fisica, poneva li principii de le cose naturali lo pari e lo dispari, considerando tutte le cose esser numero. L'altra proprietade del Sole ancor si vede nel numero, del quale è l'Arismetrica: che l'occhio de lo 'ntelletto nol può mirare; però che 'l numero quant'è in sé considerato, è infinito, e questo non potemo noi intendere. (*Conv.* II, xiii, 15–19; emphasis mine)

[The heaven of the Sun may be compared to Arithmetic on account of two properties: *the first is that it is from the Sun's light that all other stars draw theirs; the other is that the eye cannot gaze on it.* These two properties are found in Arithmetic, too, for by its light all the sciences are illuminated, since all of their subjects are to some extent studied from a numerical perspective, and progress in the study of these subjects is always made with the help of numbers. The subject of natural science, for instance, is mobile objects, which by definition has the property of infinity; further, natural science concentrates primarily on the study of the fundamental constitutive principles of natural things, of which there are three, namely, matter, privation, and form, which are also characterized by number. It is not only the ensemble of these principles that is characterized by number, but each of them individually, as careful reflection reveals; that is why Pythagoras (as reported by Aristotle) held that the fundamental principles of natural things are even and odd, since he thought that all things actually consisted of number. The second property of the Sun is also found in number, whose science is Arithmetic: the eye of the intellect cannot gaze on this, because number, considered in its intrinsic nature, is infinite, and this we human beings cannot directly apprehend.]

As Dante is about to move in the Heaven of the Sun, which is qualitatively different from previous heavens, canto X takes the form of a new prologue, where, once again, the reader is reminded of the task ahead:

Leva dunque, lettore, all'alte ruote
  meco la vista, *dritto a quella parte
  dove l'un moto e l'altro si percuote;*
(*Par.* X, 7–9; emphasis mine)

[Lift up your eyes with me then, reader, to the lofty wheels, *directly at that part where the one motion strikes the other;*]

The invitation to the reader to lift up his eyes to the Sun and to the next set of heavens (alte ruote) seems strange at first because to look directly (dritto) at the Sun is to be blinded and not to see anything. The reader runs the same risk with Arithmetic, which is the science that corresponds to this heaven, because the intellect cannot understand the concept of 'number,' which is infinite and cannot be directly apprehended by man, who is finite: 'the eye of the intellect cannot gaze on this, because number, considered in its intrinsic nature is infinite, and this we human beings cannot directly apprehend' (*Conv.* II, xiii, 18–19).

It soon becomes clear that this apparent invitation is a warning not to read the cantos that follow 'directly' as a description of the perfect ordering and harmony of the heavens, as the first lines of canto X intimate with the imagery of the Trinity: 'Guardando nel suo Figlio con l'Amore/che l'uno e l'altro etternalmente spira' [Looking upon His Son with the love which the One and the Other eternally breathe forth] (*Par.* X, 1–2). In the heavens that God created everything revolves with perfect order, such that one cannot help but admire in it the perfection of He who created it: 'con tant'ordine fé ch'esser non puote/ senza gustar di lui chi ciò rimira' [that he who contemplates it cannot but taste of Him] (5–6). Yet this perfection exists only in God's Heavens, not in these allegorical heavens of Dante's *Paradiso*, where no such order and harmony exists. On the contrary, as Dante points out, here conflict rules: 'l'un moto e l'altro si percuote' [one motion strikes the other] (9).

The problem in these heavens, and the reason for the conflict, is greed, once again a desire to satisfy earthly and material needs, which tips the heavens off their orbit towards earth rather than towards God.

> Vedi come da indi *si dirama*
> *l'oblico cerchio* che i pianeti porta,
> *per soddisfare al mondo che li chiama.*
> (*Par.* X, 13–15; emphasis mine)

> [See how from there the circle *strays obliquely* that bears the planets *to satisfy the world which calls for them*.]

The last line, 'to satisfy the world which calls them,' alludes 'obliquely' to the attraction that the earth exerted on the characters that populate these heavens and the reasons for their straying (dirama) from the right path of spiritual fulfilment. This conflict, which is at the heart of Dante's critique of the Church, applies most notably to the Heaven of the Sun, which we are about to read, and to the religious orders of Dominicans and Franciscans.

The purpose of the canto's prologue is to alert the reader to Dante's approach in these cantos – 'l'arte/ di quel maestro' [that master's art] (10–11). Since these heavens are not perfect, as they appear to be, but are 'oblique' (oblico) (14), so these cantos should be read obliquely rather than 'directly' (dritto), in order to fully understand Dante's critique of these religious orders. This is the purpose of the next address to the reader, which recalls *Inferno* I and reminds us of the objectives of the *Commedia*, and the Veltro's mandate to nourish the reader with love, wisdom, and virtue.

> Or ti riman, lettor, sovra 'l tuo banco,
> dietro pensando a ciò che si preliba,
> s'esser vuoi lieto assai prima che stanco.

> Messo t'ho innanzi: *omai per te ti ciba;*
> *ché a sé torce tutta la mia cura*
> *quella materia ond'io son fatto scriba.*
> (*Par.* X, 22–6; emphasis mine)

[Stay now, reader, on your bench, thinking over this of which you have a foretaste, and you shall have much delight before you are weary; I have set before you, *now feed yourself, for the subject of which I am made the scribe bends all my care.*]

The mission of the Veltro and of the DXV is to provide, by means of a critique of Church and Empire, the vital nourishment which in the first canto is stated as 'sapienza, amore e virtute' [wisdom, love and virtue] (*Inf.* I, 104), which, from the *Convivio* on, is Dante's main objective in the *Commedia*.

* * *

The Heaven of the Sun, which is compared to Arithmetic, takes up cantos X to XIV. As the Sun is the main planet that with its light illuminates all other planets, so Arithmetic is the first of the sciences of the Quadrivium because number is basic to all other sciences. Appropriately, in the Heaven of the Sun, Dante deals with religious orders, theologians, and doctors of the Church, who, like the Sun and Arithmetic, are responsible for bringing the light of God's truth to men, and on whose example all Christianity depends.

The first example of this 'oblique' approach is evident in Thomas Aquinas' criticism of his own order. In identifying himself to Dante as a Dominican, Thomas suggests that his order has become lax and more preoccupied with worldly care:

> Io fui delli agni della santa greggia
>   che Domenico mena per cammino
> u' ben s'impingua se non si vaneggia.
> (*Par.* X, 94–7)

[I belonged to the lambs of the holy flock that Dominic leads on the path where there is good fattening if they do not stray.]

We shall return to these lines later, but it should be clear for the moment that Thomas' criticism of the Dominicans is not confined to a general statement, but extends also to some of the doctors of the church that he mentions. Besides Albertus Magnus and himself [e io Thomas d'Aquino] (*Par.* X, 99), there is Francesco Graziano (104), Peter Lombard (107), Dionysius the Aeropagite (115), Paulus Orosius (119), Saint Augustin (indirectly) (120), Boethius (125), Isidore (131), the Venerable Bede (131), Richard of St Victor (131), and, finally, concluding the list and the crown, on Thomas' left is Siger of Brabant (136).

The presence of Siger has always been viewed as problematic because it is well-known that he and Thomas quarrelled in life. In his *De unitate intellectus,* Thomas questioned Siger's heretical and Averroistic theses. Siger replied with *De anima,* where he conceded in part to Thomas' criticism but also reiterated his heterodox rationalist doctrine (see Sapegno). In fact, Thomas' introduction of Siger, as one who carried heavy thoughts and wished for death to relieve him of them – 'è 'l lume d'uno spirto che 'n pensieri/gravi a morir li parve venir tardo:/essa è la luce etterna di Sigieri' [is the light of a spirit to whom, in his grave thoughts, death seemed slow in coming] (*Par.* X,134–6) – is meant to be read literally, as an example of 'oblique' criticism of Siger. Through Thomas, Dante is criticizing Siger's untenable theses and his rigidly deterministic views. Siger, as is well-known, held a theory of 'double truth' (doppia verità), which meant that what he could deny as a believer he could defend as a philosopher (see Sapegno). Dante makes fun of Siger's dubious and straw-like ideas when Thomas mentions that he argued his 'enviable' theories in the 'street of straw': 'che leggendo nel vico delli strami,/sillogizzò invidiosi veri' [who lecturing in the Street of Straw, demonstrated invidious truths] (137–8), an 'oblique' reference to 'la rue du Fouarre,' which means 'street of straw,' where Siger taught theology in Paris. Similarly, Siger's 'enviable truths' are not meant to be taken as ideas to be envied, but rather, ideas concocted by Siger's envy to bring damage to others.

A condemnation of syllogistic reasoning of any kind, like that of Siger, is the subject of the apostrophe at the beginning of the next canto.

O insensata cura de' mortali,
  quanto son difettivi sillogismi
  quei che ti fanno in basso batter l'ali!
(*Par.* XI, 1–3)

[O insensate care of mortals, how false is the reasoning that makes you beat your wings in downward flight!]

Dante condemns this mode of argumentation by syllogism because of the way words can be easily manipulated, as in Siger's case, to demonstrate the validity of any thesis in order to advance one's own devious and unscrupulous ambitions, rather than the truth.

> Chi dietro a iura, e chi ad aforismi
>   sen giva, e chi seguendo sacerdozio,
>   e chi regnar per forza o per sofismi,
> e chi rubare, e chi civil negozio;
>   chi nel diletto della carne involto
>   s'affaticava, e chi si dava all'ozio.
> (*Par.* XI, 4–9)

[One was going after the laws, another after the *Aphorisms*, one was pursuing priesthood, and one dominion by force or craft, and another plunder, and another civil business, one was moiling, caught in the pleasures of the flesh, and another was giving himself to idleness.]

Dante lists lawyers, doctors, priests, and monarchs, who rule by force or by deception, and thieves, businessmen, the lustful, and the indolent. All those people, in other words, who behind the appearance of reason and truth seek to advance their greed or vice.

* * *

Thomas Aquinas continues his explanation by taking up two points that have created a doubt in Dante's mind: his criticism of the Dominican Order, and the statement that none was wiser than Solomon. Thomas also points to his own role as the one who will introduce and praise St Francis, who, with St Dominic, is the other Prince of the Church, 'due principi' (*Par.* XI, 35), chosen by Divine Providence to guide the Church so that it would not stray in its ministry. Similarly, in *Paradiso* XII, the Franciscan St Bonaventure returns the favour and sings the praise of St Dominic. Both of them, in their turn, criticize their order for not living up to the standards set by their founders.

The exchange between Dominicans and Franciscans has always been seen as a 'gesture of exquisite courtesy, a high point of the courtly sensitivity of heaven' (see Sapegno), which is what one would expect in *Paradiso*. But, as we have seen so far, this is never the case, and although the souls we meet occupy a place in Paradise, Dante still denounces their past, earthly flaws. This is especially the case for the souls in the Heaven of the Sun, who like the Sun and Arithmetic, were supposed to provide, with their teachings and exemplary lives, a model of Christian life to follow. Since this is hardly the case with the Dominican and the Franciscan orders, the praise of one order for the other cannot be understood as an instance of goodwill typical of the souls of Paradise, but as a form of 'oblique' punishment, in the mode of irony, to which Dante subjects first Thomas and then Bonaventure, as well as their respective orders. Although it was common practice on the birthday of one of the two founders to praise the other, neither Thomas nor Bonaventure would be caught dead praising the other rival order, or even criticizing their own order. The same type of criticism goes for Saint Francis and Saint Dominic, whose praise by a member of the opposite order can also be read as an example of that oblique, or ironic, criticism that characterizes the Heaven of the Sun, as I will try to show.

Cantos XI and XII, which deal with the praise of St Francis and St Dominic, are only apparently symmetrical, despite an effort to make them appear so. The structure of the cantos seems parallel as Thomas praises St Francis and then criticizes the Dominicans, and Bonaventure praises St Dominic and then criticizes the Franciscans. The two princes (due principi) of the Church (*Par.* XI, 35) are even said to be interchangeable. When Thomas speaks of St Francis, he is also speaking of St Dominic, since they both shared the same goal: 'De l'un dirò, però che d'amendue/si dice l'un pregiando, quale uom prende,/perch'ad un fine fuor l'opere sue' [I shall tell of the one, since to praise one, whichever we take, is to speak of both; for their labours were to one end] (40–2). And just as the praise of St Francis is followed by a critique of the Dominican Order by a Dominican, the praise of St Dominic is followed by a critique of the Franciscan Order by a Franciscan.

Despite these similarities the episodes differ somewhat, and not only because St Francis is 'tutto serafico in ardore' [all seraphic in ardour] (*Par.* XI, 37) while St. Dominic is 'per sapienza in terra fue/di cherubica luce uno splendore' [for wisdom, was on earth a splendour of cherubic light] (38–9), but because one is a champion at doing and the other at saying: 'con due campioni, al cui fare, al cui dire/lo popol disviato si raccorse' [by two champions at whose deeds and words the scattered people rallied] (*Par.* XII, 44–5). The similarities and differences of the two orders are comparable to Echo and Narcissus, who are recalled in the description of the coloured and parallel arches of the two crowns in *Paradiso* XII:

> Come si volgon per tenera nube
> *due archi parallei e con colori,*
> quando Iunone a sua ancella iube,
> nascendo di quel d'entro quel di fori,
> *a guisa di parlar di quella vaga*
> *ch'amor consunse come sol vapori.*
> (*Par.* XII, 10–15; emphasis mine)

[As *two parallel arches* and of like colour bend through thin clouds when Juno commands her handmaid, the outer born of the inner – *like the voice of that wandering nymph whom love consumed as the sun does vapours.*]

Where there is Echo there is Narcissus, and where there is St Francis there is St Dominic. 'Degno è che, dov'è l'un, l'altro s'induca;/sì che, com'elli ad una militaro,/ così la gloria loro insieme luca' [It is fitting that where the one is, the other should be brought in, so that, as they fought for one end, their glory should shine together] (*Par.* XII, 34–6). And just as Echo and Narcissus are examples of the mystification of language and image, respectively, so are St Dominic and St Francis.

The linguistic mystification which is Echo is well-known. She is condemned by Juno to repeat everything that she hears, but only the last words of what she hears. Echo, thus, informs the figure of St Dominic and the entire canto XII, which begins with a reference to Echo and her linguistic limitations.

> Sí tosto come *l'ultima parola*
> la benedetta fiamma per dir tolse,
> a rotar cominciò *la santa mola.*
> (*Par.* XII, 1–3; emphasis mine)

[As soon as the blessed flame took up *the last word* the *holy millstone* began to turn.]

The reference to 'santa mola' is, indirectly, to St Dominic, whose life and whose achievements are listed by St Bonaventure in this canto. The reference in line 1 to 'l'ultima parola' is a reference to Echo and to the fact that she repeats only the last words of what she hears. But the allusion, in this case, is also to the last words of the previous canto, 'se non si vaneggia' [if they do not stray] (*Par.* XI, 140), which concludes Thomas' speech and the canto.

One of Dante's doubts expressed at the beginning of *Par.* XI (22–5) refers to Thomas' statement 'u' ben s'impingua se non si vaneggia' (*Par.* X, 96), about the Dominicans, who will receive spiritual nourishment unless they deviate from the practice set out by St Dominic. In his reply, Thomas lunges into an account of the life of St Francis, at the end of which he mentions St Dominic as St Francis' only 'worthy colleague' (degno collega fu) (118–19), and then proceeds with what appears to be a critique of the Dominicans:

> e questo fu il nostro patriarca;
>   per che, qual segue lui com'el comanda,
>   discerner puoi che buone merce carca.
> (*Par.* XI, 121–3)
>
> [and such was our Patriarch; from which you may perceive that he who follows him as he commands carries good merchandise.]

Those who follow the dictates of St Dominic will reap their reward. Here the conceit is that the good Dominican will be heavy with spiritual merchandise to dispense to the world. But the metaphor for spiritual nourishment, so central to the *Convivio* and to the *Commedia*, which alludes to the spiritual nourishment that the two princes of the Church, through their order, ought to provide their flock, turns literally into food to refer to the corruption of the Dominican Order, which, instead of feeding on spiritual nourishment, has now become greedy and gluttonous:

> Ma 'l suo peculio di nova vivanda
>   è fatto ghiotto, sì ch'esser non puote
>   che per diversi salti non si spanda.
> (*Par.* XI, 124–6)
>
> [But his flock has grown so greedy of new fare that it must needs scatter through wild pastures.]

The more the flock wanders away from the established order and the precepts of St Dominic, the more it becomes spiritually impoverished:

> e quanto le sue pecore remote
>   e vagabunde più da esso vanno,

> più tornano all'ovil di latte vote.
> (*Par.* XI, 125–7)

[and the farther his sheep go wandering from him the emptier of milk they return to the fold.]

The more the flock abandons the right way the more it lacks the spiritual nourishment it should be getting and should be passing on to others. Only a few still follow the rule of St Dominic, but these act more out of fear than out of choice: 'Ben son di quelle che temono 'l danno / e stringonsi al pastor; ma son sí poche' [Some there are, indeed, that for fear of harm keep close to the shepherd] (*Par.* XI, 130–1). Thomas's critique of the Dominicans wants to serve as a corrective for the present state of the order. If you have paid attention, he tells Dante, you will understand the purpose of the rebuke:

> Or se le mie parole non son fioche
>   e *se la tua audienza è stata attenta*,
>   se ciò ch'è detto alla mente rivoche,
> in parte fia la tua voglia contenta,
>   *perchè vedrai la pianta onde sì scheggia*,
>   *e vedra' il corregger che argomenta*
> 'U' ben s'impingua, se non si vaneggia.'
>   (*Par.* XI, 133–9; emphasis mine)

[If my words are not obscure and *if you have listened carefully*, if you recall to mind what I said, your desire shall in part be satisfied and you *shall see how the plant is wasted and you will see the corrected argument*, 'Where there is good fattening, if they do not stray.']

Thomas' conclusion repeats the earlier statement of *Paradiso* X (96), which made the spreading of St Dominic's teachings conditional on the strict observance of his rule by his followers: 'u' ben s'impingua se non si vaneggia.' When the statement is repeated, however, Echo-like, only the second part is emphasized by the inclusion of a comma (,): 'u' ben s'impingua, se non si vaneggia.' The emphasis is now placed on 'se non si vaneggia,' which points to the error of the Dominicans, who have, in fact, strayed from the principles set by St Dominic. But Thomas' criticism, or Dante's, is also meant for the Franciscans, not only because of the similarities between the two orders, and the two 'princes' and two principles (principi), but also because of the ambiguity in Thomas' speech, which speaks first of St Francis, then of St Dominic, and then refers to his followers (qual segue lui com'el comanda), leaving open the possibility that it applies to the followers of both orders. Ultimately, Dante's critique applies to the two princes of the Church, or to the principles of the two orders, as the following lines appear to imply:

> Degno è che, dov'è l'un, l'altro s'induca;
>   sí che, com'elli ad una militaro,
>   cosí la gloria loro insieme luca.
> (*Par.* XII, 34–6)

> [It is fitting that where the one is the other should be brought in, so that, as they fought for one end, their glory should shine together.]

Here the conceit is clear. These verses not only express the idea that speaking of St Francis, one is also speaking of St Dominic, but they are also an indirect condemnation of their leadership, 'com'elli ad una militaro.' They both deserve the (little) glory that their followers are earning them (cosí la gloria loro insieme luca).

In fact, St Bonaventure's critique of the Franciscans reiterates a similar critique in demonstrating that the Franciscans have similarly abandoned the way set by their leader: 'Ma l'orbita che fe' la parte somma/di sua circunferenza, è derelitta' [But the track made by the topmost part of its rim is abandoned] (*Par.* XII, 112–13). The followers of St Francis are so removed from the path, which the saint opened for them, that instead of moving forward, they are moving backward: 'La sua famiglia, che si mosse dritta/coi piedi alle sue orme, è tanto volta, che quel dinanzi a quel di retro gitta' [His family, which started out straightforward with their feet in his footprints, is so turned around that who is ahead throws to who is behind] (115–17). And just as with the Dominicans, there are only a few Franciscans who still follow the rules of the order: 'Ben dico, chi cercasse a foglio a foglio ?/ nostro volume, ancor troveria carta/ u' leggerebbe "I' mi son quel ch'i' soglio" ' [I admit that whoever would search our volume leaf by leaf, he would still find a page where he might read, 'I am what I always was'] (121–3). The reference is to the Franciscan Rule, approved by Pope Innocent III in 1210, and to the fact that very few Franciscans in Dante's day followed it.

Bonaventure's praise of St Dominic and critique of the Franciscans follows the specular structure of Thomas' speech, or almost. There is no apparent condemnation on the part of Bonaventure of a fellow Franciscan, as Thomas criticized his rival, Siger, except for Bonaventure's mention of his arch rival Abbot Joachim da Fiore ('Giovacchino'), who had the gift of prophecy, 'di spirito profetico dotato' [endowed with a spirit of prophecy]. The line, however, is consistent with Thomas's critique of Siger, and must be read ironically. In fact, Joachim prophesied the coming of a world morally and socially regenerated (Sapegno). Although many critics thought Dante shared these same ideals, it is clear that what Joachin prophesied has not come to pass, hence Bonaventure's irony.

The end of Bonaventure's speech is shrouded in mystery. The lines have been thought to form a coda to Bonaventure's admission that he was moved to speak of St Dominic after hearing Thomas' speech on St Francis:

Ad inveggiar cotanto paladino
  mi mosse *l'infiammata cortesia*
  di fra Tommaso e *'l discreto latino.*
  (*Par.* XII, 142–4; emphasis mine)

[The glowing courtesy and *discrete Latin* of St Thomas moved me to praise such a knight.]

The line 'discreto Latino' has created much confusion. It is usually taken to mean 'assennato discorso' (Sapegno), and is usually translated in English as 'the well-judged discourse' (Singleton). This reading has always supposed that Bonaventure, in the spirit of Paradise and reconciliation, was being polite to Thomas, but it is clear, at least in my critical reading, that this is not the case. It would seem, instead, that Bonaventure is taking on Thomas, perhaps for having implicated the Franciscan Order in his critique of the Dominicans. The allusion to Thomas' 'infiammata cortesia,' which is usually interpreted positively as it is in English when it is translated as 'glowing courtesy,' can be read as meaning the opposite, as 'inflamed courtesy,' in the sense of angry and critical. The metaphors employed by Bonaventure, such as 'inveggiar cotanto paladino,' give a real sense of a duel that is taking place. According to Pagliaro (see Sapegno) 'inveggiar' can also mean to 'chiamare in campo' 'sfidare,' that is, to challenge. Although, it may be clear why Bonaventure wants it out with Thomas, it is not clear how and when he manages to get back at him. The key seems to be in the phrase 'discreto latino,' which, besides insulting Thomas that his Latin is 'average,' can also allude to the discretionary use made of Latin, as when an accusation is made in Latin rather than in *volgare* (Italian), as a form of discretion and concealment. The only instance of Latin in the canto is in Bonaventure's speech when speaking of St Dominic, when he states that Dominic in his application to the Church had not asked permission to give out in charity a third or half of the money received. Bonaventure says in Latin that he did not ask for the 'tithes' (decimas), which belong to God's poor.

> non dispensar o due o tre per sei,
>   non la fortuna di prima vacante,
>   non *decimas, quae sunt pauperum Dei,*
> addimandò,
>   (*Par.* XII, 91–4; emphasis mine)

[he asked not to dispense two or three for six, not for the fortune of the first vacancy, not for *the tithes which belong to God's poor*]

Bonaventure's insistence on the fact that St Dominic never asked to keep the money that belonged to the poor, implies, obliquely, that this is now the practice of the Dominicans, which is how they have swayed from the rule of their founder, and have now become 'materially fat' (u' ben s'impingua). By further associating Thomas with his discreet Latin, the implication is that Thomas himself is not exempt from having grown fat on the money that belonged to the poor. Bonaventure is repaying Thomas for having insinuated earlier that the Franciscans like the Dominicans have equally gone astray, just as they have: 'Se non si vaneggia' [If they don't stray] (*Par.* XI, 139).

According to Bonaventure, the problem afflicting the Franciscans is their leadership, as they are torn between Ubertino da Casale, who would like to tighten the rules of the order, and Matteo d'Acquasparta, who would like to depart from the rules: 'non fia da Casal né d'Acquasparta,/là onde vegnon tali alla scrittura,/ch'uno la fugge, e altro la coarta' [they are not those from Casale or from Acquasparta, where one shirks from the Rule and the other narrows it] (*Par.* XII, 124–6). The Franciscans might have this problem, but they are not as bad as the Dominicans.

* * *

Whereas the Dominicans are depicted on the side of Echo and are characterized by a linguistic flaw, the Franciscans are on the side of Narcissus and are characterized by an image flaw. This is made clear in *Paradiso* XIII, which appropriately begins with an invitation to the reader to imagine (imagini), and to keep the image firmly and solidly, like a rock,

> Imagini chi bene intender cupe
>   quel ch'i' vidi or – e ritegna l'image,
>   mentre ch'io dico, come ferma rupe.
>   (*Par.* XIII, 1–3)

> [Let him imagine, who would rightly understand what I saw now – and let him hold the image, while I speak, firm as a rock.]

While the appeal to the reader is to imagine the scene of the two constellations of stars that Dante is seeing, the apostrophe has deeper implications, since the canto which is about to unfold has to do, precisely, with maintaining the image of something imagined, which has nothing to do with the reality of the way things are.

After resolving Dante's first doubt, concerning 'u' ben s'impingua se non si vaneggia,' Thomas wants to resolve his second doubt, which he raised in canto X, as to why Solomon is the wisest of men.

> entro v'è l'alta mente u' sí profondo
>   saver fu messo, che se 'l vero è vero
>   a veder tanto non surse il secondo.
>   (*Par.* X, 111–13)

> [within it is the lofty mind to whom was given wisdom so deep that, if the truth be true, there never arose a wiser one.]

Dante's doubt is not as disconcerting as is the presence of Solomon among a long list of Dominicans. Commentators, on the whole, do not seem to be bothered by it. For instance, Sapegno thinks his presence is justified, as he is the wisest among wise Dominicans. The fact remains, however, that when Thomas introduces his fellow Dominicans, Solomon is not one of them. The apparent reasons for Solomon's presence are made clear in canto XIII when Thomas confirms that he is the wisest of men, or at least the wisest king. And just as Dante's earlier doubt helps us understand, obliquely, the Dominicans' status as Echo, Solomon's wisdom can be said to concern the Franciscans' status as Narcissus.

In his reply, Thomas states that Solomon asked God for wisdom because he was a king and wanted to be a fair ruler, and the Lord gladly granted it to him: 'ch'el fu re che chiese senno/acciò che re sufficiente fosse' [he was a king who asked for wisdom that he might be fit to be a king] (*Par.* XIII, 95–6). Yet in Solomon's case we are not concerned with the scholastic wisdom that would allow him to understand the essence of number or to reason logically through syllogisms (*Par.* XIII, 97–102). The type of wisdom Solomon asked for was the wisdom to rule wisely, which goes by the name of 'regal prudenza' [royal prudence] (*Par.* XIII, 104), and this is what God gave him. In the Old Testament (1 Kings 2: 12) we read that God said to Solomon: 'Behold, I give you a wise and discerning mind, so that none like you has been before you and none like you shall arise after you.'

Thomas wants the reader to take this image of Solomon for granted and to keep it as a rock (come ferma rupe), or as lead on our feet ('piombo a' piedi') (*Par.* XIII, 112), as we move further in the uncertainty of contradictory evidence: 'per farti muover lento com'uom lasso/ e al sí e al no che tu non vedi' [to make you slow, like a weary man, in moving either to the yes or to the no, where you do not see clearly] (113–14). Thomas warns us from making hasty judgments and advises us to proceed slowly before committing ourselves to a yes or a no. In an apostrophe to the reader on how to read, he criticizes the reading of Scripture by the early heretics, who made the Old Testament say the opposite of what it said: 'e quelli stolti/che furon come spade alle Scritture/in render torti li diritti volti' [and those fools who were to the Scriptures like swords that give back the natural face distorted] (128–9). Finally, he warns us against making hasty judgments because we cannot always predict what will happen, since events can turn out differently from what we had anticipated:

Non creda donna Berta e ser Martino,
   per vedere un furare, altro offerere,
   vederli dentro al consiglio divino;
ché quel può surgere, e quel può cadere.'
   (*Par.* XIII, 139–42)

[Let not Bertha or Martin, when they see one steal and one making an offering, believe they see them within the divine counsel; for one may rise and the other may fall.']

The issue at stake is the working of Divine Providence, 'consiglio divino (*Par.* XIII, 141), which baffles the common man ('donna Berta' and 'ser Martino'), who believes he can guess how divine justice works. In Solomon's case the issue appears to be resolved. He is not wiser than either Adam or God. He is just the wisest king, and his wisdom, granted him by God, is of a practical nature that allows him to rule wisely.

However, the issue of whether Solomon is wiser than Adam or God is just a pretext that conceals an even more important point. The issue of how the truth can be distorted in this case does not refer only to Solomon's wisdom but to the broader issue of Solomon the man. When we read the story of Solomon we discover that although he had the reputation of being a very wise king, his great success, which brought him enormous wealth and 700 wives and 300 concubines, also brought about his downfall. Although God had told Solomon to have nothing to do with other religions, his wives and concubines who came from different lands and wanted to worship their own deities persuaded him to erect temples to their gods. The situation escalated to such proportions that it was said of Solomon that 'his heart was no longer entirely of God, his Lord, as it had been of David, his father.' Since Solomon went back on the promise he had made to God, the Lord told him that He would take the reign away from him, but only after his death out of respect for his father, David (I Kings 11: 11–13).

As commentators remind us, Solomon's salvation was an issue at the time of Dante, namely, whether he had gone to Heaven for his wisdom or to Hell for his lasciviousness. Dante seems to resolve the question by placing him in *Paradiso* in this canto. But Thomas' insistence that we keep firm this image of Solomon as a wise king is suspect because it is aimed at keeping the reader from investigating further the baser and more unfortunate details of his life. In fact, there is no doubt that Dante wants to allude to this other aspect of Solomon's life, when, in introducing him, Thomas places emphasis not on his wisdom but on his capacity to love:

> La quinta luce, ch'è tra noi più bella,
>   *spira di tale amor*, che tutto 'l mondo
>   là giù ne gola di saper novella:
> entro v'è l'alta mente u' sí profondo
>   saver fu messo, che *se 'l vero è vero*.
>   (*Par.* X, 109–13; emphasis mine)

[The fifth light, which is the most beautiful among us, *breathes from such a love* that all the world below hungers for news of it; within it is the lofty mind to which was given wisdom so deep that, *if the truth be truth*, there never arose a second such vision.]

Solomon breathes love; his wisdom was just given to him. If the truth be told, or, as Thomas puts it, 'perché paia ben ciò che non pare' [so that it appears clear what is obscure] *(Par.* XIII, 91), Solomon should have gone to Hell, but he is in Paradise. This is the 'consiglio divino' that baffles the common man, 'donna Berta' and 'ser Martino,' who do not understand why Solomon is in Heaven. Ordinary people cannot guess God's will and why one man is saved and another damned to Hell: 'ché quel può surgere, e quel può cadere' [for one may rise and the other may fall] (142).

The image that Thomas wants us to keep of Solomon is after all what we get from the Gospel and the Book of Kings, which shifts the punishment of Solomon onto his son Roboamo, preferring to leave the image of the wise King Solomon untarnished. However, the presence of Solomon amongst the Dominicans is not only supposed to denounce this aberration, but in insisting on the importance of maintaining a 'good' image it is also a critique of the Franciscan and Dominican Orders, and of the 'good' image they have created for themselves, which is radically different from the truth.

In *Paradiso* XIII, Dante criticizes the concept of image as a narcissistic flaw with no base in reality. This is not the case, however, for the poem we are reading, where the author is always aware of the discrepancy between image and reality:

ma la natura la dà sempre scema,
   similmente operando all'artista
c'ha l'abito dell'arte e man che trema.
(Par. XIII, 76–8)

[but nature always gives it defectively, working like the artist who has the skill of his art and a hand that trembles.]

Hence Dante's warning against making rush judgments – 'Non sien le genti, ancor, troppo sicure/ a giudicar' [So also let not the people be too sure in judging] *(Par.* XIII, 130–1), which applies in general to this Heaven of the Sun, where nothing is ever what it seems to be, and where an image is never the reflection of an inner truth, but always a form of concealment. In the Heaven of the Sun, the punitive action of the DXV takes the form of a critique of religious orders, and of the greed and corruption that have brought about their decline.

5 Heaven of Mars: Music (XV–XVII)

E lo cielo di Marte si può comparare a la Musica per due proprietadi; l'una si è la sua più bella relazione, ché, annumerando li cieli mobili, da qualunque si comincia o da l'infimo o dal sommo, esso cielo di Marte è lo quinto, esso è lo mezzo di tutti, cioè de li primi, de li secondi, de li terzi e de li quarti. L'altra si è che esso, (sì come dice Tolomeo nel Quadripartito), (e) ss(o) Marte dissecca e arde le cose, perché lo suo calore è simile a quello del fuoco; e questo è quello per che esso pare affocato di colore, quando più e quando meno, secondo la spessezza e raritade de li vapori che 'l seguono, li quali per lor medesimi molte volte s'accendono, sì come nel primo de la Metaura è determinato. E però dice Albumasar che l'accendimento di questi vapori significa morte di regi e trasmutamento di regni; però che sono effetti de la segnoria di Marte; e Seneca dice però che, ne la morte d' Augusto imperatore, vide in alto una palla di fuoco; e in Fiorenza, nel principio de la sua destruzione, veduta fu ne l'aere, in figura d'una croce, grande quantità di questi vapori, seguaci de la stella di Marte. E queste due proprietadi sono ne la Musica, la quale è tutta relativa, sì come si vede ne le parole armonizzate e ne li canti, de' quali tanto più dolce armonia resulta, quanto più la relazione è bella; la quale in essa scienza massimamente è bella, perché massimamente in essa s'intende. Ancora: la Musica trae a sé li spiriti umani, che quasi sono principalmente vapori del cuore, sì che quasi cessano da ogni operazione; sì è l'anima intera, quando l'ode, e la virtù di tutti quasi corre a lo spirito sensibile, che riceve lo suono. (*Conv.* II, 201–4)

[The heaven of Mars may be compared to Music on account of two properties: the first is that its relationship to the other moving heavens is the most beautiful, for if we count these beginnings at either the lowest or the highest, the Heaven of Mars comes fifth, and so midway between all the others; that is, midway between the first two, the second two, the third two, and the fourth two. The second property is that, as Ptolemy says in the *Tetrabiblos*, this Heaven of Mars dries things and burns them, because its heat is like that of fire; for this reason it has the colour of something on fire, deeper and lighter at various times depending on the density or rarity of the vapours which follow it, which often spontaneously burst into flames, as is demonstrated in the *Meterroics*. Consequently, Albumasar says that the flaring of these vapours signals the death of kings and the transfer of royal authority, since these effects are under the dominion of Mars: this explains why Seneca says that at the time of the Emperor Augustus' death he saw a ball of fire in the sky, and why, too, in Florence, at the onset of its destruction, there was seen in the air, in the form of a cross, a great quantity of these vapours which follow the star of Mars. These two properties are found in Music, too, for Music is entirely a matter of relationships, as is evident in speech, in respect of poetry, and in songs, for the sweetness of the harmony created by any one of these works is in proportion to the beauty of the relationship within it; it is in this science that we principally find the beauty specific to relationship, for relationship is its principal concern. Furthermore, Music draws to itself the various spirits in a person (which may be said to consist mainly of vapours of the heart) to the extent that they almost cease to carry out any of their functions: to such a degree does the soul form a single entity when it hears Music, that the power in all the spirits rushes, as it were, to the sensitive spirit, which receives the sound.]

The Heaven of Mars can be called the heaven of Florence, as Mars, the god of war, was once Florence's major divinity, replaced later by St John the Baptist, and occupies the mid-point in Dante's *Paradiso*, as the planet Mars does. The key symbol of these cantos is the Cross, formed by two converging Milky Ways, in the middle of which one can discern the image of Christ, "n quella croce lampeggiava Cristo' [in that Cross was flashing Christ] (*Par.* XIV, 104). This is the Cross of the crusading warriors for Christ, among whom is Cacciaguida, who followed it to defeat the unbelievers, 'chi prende sua croce e segue Cristo' [who takes up his cross and follows Christ] (106). It is also the Cross that marks the origin and downfall of Florence: 'in Florence, at the onset of its destruction, there was seen in the air, in the form of a cross, a great quantity of these vapours which follow the star of Mars' (*Conv.* II, 201–4).

Heaven of Mars: Music 79

The Cross is made up of minute bodies of light that move across and up and down like dust particles that move in and out of the light.

> Di corno in corno e tra la cima e 'l basso
>   si movien lumi, scintillando forte
>   nel congiugnersi insieme e nel trapasso:
> così si veggion qui diritte e torte,
>   veloci e tarde, *rinovando vista*,
>   le minuzie de' corpi, lunghe e corte,
> moversi per lo raggio *onde si lista*
>   *tal volta l'ombra che, per sua difesa,*
>   *la gente con ingegno e arte acquista.*
>   (*Par.* XIV, 109–17; emphasis mine)

[From horn to horn and between the summit and the base, lights were moving that sparkled brightly as they met and passed; so we see here, direct and athwart, swift and slow, *changing appearances*, the particles of matter, long and short, moving through the beam that *sometimes streaks the shade which men devise with cunning and skill for their own protection.*]

The movement of the bodies of light along the Cross provides an important clue to the interpretation of these cantos. Just as a sunbeam exposes dust particles in a dark room, the light of Dante's critique exposes the flaws of those who are trying to hide them with their art and their wit, 'con ingegno e arte.' This is what is implied by the term 'rinovando vista,' which means, literally, 'renewing sight,' but not in the sense of 'changing appearances,' as it is usually translated, but in the sense of bringing to light something that was not apparent at first.

The same technique is provided by sound and is stated as a contradiction. Just as the sound of many instruments chimes sweetly for someone who does not catch the tune, so is the melody sweet that holds the pilgrim in rapture, though he cannot follow the hymn.

> E come giga e arpa, in tempra tesa
>   di molte corde, fa dolce tintinno
>   a tal da cui la nota non è intesa,
> così da' lumi che lì m'apparinno
>   s'accogliea per la croce una melode

che mi rapiva, sanza intender l'inno.
(*Par.* XIV, 118–23)

[And as viol and harp, strung with many cords in harmony, chime sweetly for one who does not catch the tune, so from the lights that appeared to me there a melody gathered through the cross which held me rapt, though I could not follow the hymn.]

Commentators have tried to make sense of this analogy by inserting an 'even if,' to imply that the sound is sweet 'even if' one does not catch the tune, but the lines seem to allude to quite a different situation. The first term of the comparison wants to indicate that the chimes are sweet 'precisely because' one does not catch the tune. Likewise, the melody holds the pilgrim in rapture 'precisely because' he cannot follow the hymn. The sense of the analogy is not unlike what is said in the *Convivio* of the *canzoni*, which were appreciated for their beautiful verses and not for what they signified. In either case, if one does not understand the *canzoni*, or catch the tune, or follow the hymn, one is easily carried away by the sound. However, if one understands the meaning of what is written, or of what is being said, one is no longer carried away. This is made clear in the next example when the pilgrim hears 'Arise' and 'Conquer,' but without understanding what it means: 'Ben m'accors' io ch'elli era d'alte lode, / però ch'a me venia 'Resurgi' e 'Vinci' / come a colui che non intende e ode' [I thought that it had to be of high praise, for there came to me 'Arise' and 'Conquer,' as one hears without understanding] (*Par.* XIV, 124–6). Commentators explain that these lines refer to Christ triumphant over death and hell. Singleton quotes Grandgent that this is 'evidently a triumphal hymn to Christ, sung by the knights of the Cross.' The meaning, however, is much more ominous because the words 'Arise' and 'Conquer' may be a call to arms such as crusaders might employ for the defence of Christ's sepulchre, or soldiers for other military undertakings such as a civil war, and the words can sound sweet only if one doesn't understand them. When we do understand them, by a reading that sheds light on the particles of dust like a sunbeam, they can point to impending doom or to the downfall of a city.

Canto XIV, the introductory canto of the Heaven of Mars, sets the parameters for what constitutes the 'sunbeam' that will make it possible to interpret and understand the next two cantos. This 'sunlight' can be summed up as a distrust for what appears to be sweet and harmonious, but which, on analysis, turns out to be a façade that conceals a more ominous reality that must be exposed. This is the light of an 'oblique' mode of reading, which enables the reader to gain an insight into Dante's critique of the civil war that ravaged Florence from its origins and brought about its undoing, concealed behind the façade of an harmonious and moving family reunion between Dante and his great-great-grandfather Cacciaguida, which parallels the meeting between Anchises and Aeneas.

* * *

The opening lines of *Paradiso* XV provide a first example of this indirect critique. Since right love 'amor che dirittamente spira' [love that breathes directly] (*Par.* XV, 2) only exists in heaven, the real focus of the passage becomes greed, 'cupidità,' love for worldly and material things:

> Benigna volontade in che si liqua
>   sempre l'amor che drittamente spira,
>   come cupidità fa nella iniqua.
> (*Par.* XV, 1–3)

> [Gracious will, in which right love always resolves itself, as does greed into evil.]

This is the love for what is not everlasting, 'per amor di cosa che non duri' [for love of what does not endure] (*Par.* XV, 11), and those who seek it will be deprived eternally of God's everlasting love: 'Bene è che sanza termine si doglia/ chi, per amor di cosa che non duri/ etternalmente, quello amor si spoglia' [Right it is that he should grieve without end who, for the love of what does not endure forever, robs himself of that love] (10–2).

This duality of heavenly love and earthy greed characterizes the figure of Cacciaguida, who is the only character of these cantos. The pious and magnanimous figure readers have always loved as Dante's benign ancestor corresponds only to his heavenly appearance. The earthly Cacciaguida who hides behind this façade is, on the contrary, a figure of greed and evil. The dissimulation which conceals the 'real' Cacciaguida can only be arrived at through an oblique reference that denounces him as 'Caesar,' responsible for Florence's civil wars.

A first indication that all is not well with Cacciaguida comes from the initial Virgilian reference, 'O sanguis meus,' with which Cacciaguida greets Dante.

> Sí pia l'ombra d'Anchise si porse,
> *se fede merta nostra maggior musa,*
> quando in Eliso del figlio s'accorse.
> 'O sanguis meus, o superinfusa
> gratia Dei, sicut tibi cui
> bis unquam coeli ianua reclusa?'
> Cosí quel lume:
> (*Par.* XV, 25–31; first emphasis mine)

[With such affection did Anchises' shade reach out, *if we may trust our greatest muse,* when in Elysium he noticed his son: 'O blood of mine, O lavish grace of God! To whom was heaven's gate ever twice opened, as to thee?' That light spoke thus:]

These are the words of Anchises, who in the *Aeneid* addresses the not-yet-born spirit of Julius Caesar in the hope of dissuading him from engaging in a civil war with Pompey:

> See those twin souls, resplendent in duplicate armour: now
> they're of one mind, and shall be as long as the Underworld holds them;
> But oh, if ever they reach the world above, what warfare,
> what battles and what carnage will they create between them –
> Caesar descending from Alpine strongholds, the fort Monoecus,
> his son-in-law Pompey lined up with an Eastern army against him.
> *Lads do not harden yourselves to face such terrible wars!*
> *Turn not your country's hand against your country's heart!*
> *Cast from thy hand the sword, thou blood of mine!*
> (*Proice tela manu, sanguis meus*)
> *You be the first to bury the hatchet!*
> (*Aeneid* VI, 826–35; emphasis mine)

Dante's comment as to whether we can take Virgil at his word, 'if we may trust our greatest muse,' calls attention to a possible discrepancy between Virgil's and Dante's texts. At first, in fact, there does not seem to be a similarity between the two episodes, but on reflection we realize that the two versions are quite similar. Just as Aeneas' father, Anchises, is Caesar's ancestor, so Cacciaguida is Dante's ancestor. Furthermore, since Dante is a Florentine, and Caesar, as the legend goes, is the founder of Florence, Caesar is also Dante's ancestor, and so is Anchises. In all these cases, the phrase 'sanguis meus' is applicable to Dante, though Dante is not Caesar; he is his descendent and proud of it, as we shall see. So we would have to say that we can trust Virgil, our greatest muse, but can we really? Can we trust his condemnation of Julius Caesar in *Aeneid* VI, through the persona of Anchises, as the man responsible for Rome's civil wars? And is Virgil's statement also a veiled condemnation of Augustus, who, as the adopted son of Julius Caesar, was also called Gaius Julius Caesar Augustus? But how can we trust Virgil, when, for greed and personal ambition, as Juvenal relates,[1] he wrote an epic that glorified the violence and the injustices of the Romans and of Augustus' Empire?[2]

The Roman poet that Dante trusted is Lucan, whose epic, *Pharsalia*, on the tragic civil war between Julius Caesar and Pompey he knew well and admired. Lucan's life and work is the antithesis of Virgil's. He is the poet who wrote and died for his ideals, who placed his poetry at the service of freedom and justice, and who denounced in his poetry the tyrant Nero, who was also a Caesar, at the cost of his own life. Dante gives him a seat of honour among the six greatest poets of all time, beside himself and Virgil, with Homer, Horace, and Ovid: 'e l'ultimo Lucano' [and Lucan the last one] (*Inf.* IV, 90). Lucan is mentioned directly in *Inferno* XXV, 94 ('Taccia Lucano') and in the Heaven of Mercury, as we have seen, but it is in this Heaven of Mars that his influence is most felt, albeit indirectly, since the main theme of his *Pharsalia* is also the main theme of these cantos on Florence's civil war. Lucan we can trust.

* * *

The reference to Anchises' 'sanguis meus' serves to establish a link between Caesar and Rome's civil war, as Lucan recounts it, and between Cacciaguida and the civil war that devastated Florence. By association, as I have indicated, Caesar, as the putative founder of Florence, and

---

1 For Juvenal's critique of Virgil in the *Satires* and Dante's use of it, see chapter 7 of *Readsing Dante Reading*.
2 For a more detailed critique of Virgil see chapter 3 of *Reading Dante Reading*.

Anchises as Caesar's ancestor, can both be considered Dante's ancestors, together with Cacciaguida. When Cacciaguida first meets Dante, he addresses him with Anchises' words, 'sanguis meus,' but the rest is not what Virgil wrote:

'*O sanguis meus, o superinfusa*
 gratia Dei, sicut tibi cui
 bis unquam coeli ianua reclusa?'
Cosí quel lume:
(*Par.* XV, 28–31)

Cacciaguida, as Dante's purported ancestor, is identified, ironically at first, as 'quel lume' [that light], but it is a light that hides him, as his Latin also does. His Latin, of course, not only links him to an ancient time in Florence, when Latin was spoken, but also with the figure of Caesar, with whom he is linked. His Latin is a form of concealment of his past role in Florence's civil wars, a past he tries to hide not by choice but by necessity: 'né per elezion mi si nascose/ ma per necessità' (*Par.* XV, 40–1). His connection with Caesar is also evident in Dante's use of 'voi' in addressing Cacciaguida, which was the form of address Caesar imposed on the people of Rome to show respect for his authority:

Dal 'voi' che prima a Roma s'offerie,
 in che la sua famiglia men persevra,
 ricominciaron le parole mie;
(*Par.* XVI, 10–12)

[With that You which was first used in Rome and in which her family least perseveres, my words began again;]

The 'voi-form' that present-day Romans no longer use, and which they suffered to use, was a form of address that elevated Caesar above all other men, at the same time that it humiliated those who were forced to use it. The pride and boldness inherent in the 'voi' can be seen by reflection in Dante's behaviour. Since he is a descendant of Cacciaguida, and Caesar's descendant, he is full of pride:

Io cominciai: 'Voi siete il padre mio;
 voi mi date a parlar tutta baldezza;

voi mi levate sì, *ch'i' son più ch'io*.
(*Par.* XVI, 16–18; emphasis mine)

[I began, 'You are my father, you give me full boldness to speak, you so uplift me so *that I am more than I.*]

'To be more than I' is already a sign of arrogance that reflects both Caesar's and Cacciaguida's pride at being superior to others. A sign of his superiority was already expressed earlier as his being above mortals: 'ché 'l suo concetto/al segno d'i mortal si soprapuose' [for his concept was set above the mark of mortals] (*Par.* XV, 41–2). This same arrogance can also be read in his initial Latin words to Dante: 'O superinfusa/gratia Dei, sicut tibi cui bis unquam coeli ianua recluse,' that is, 'O lavish grace of God! To whom was Heaven's gate ever twice opened, as to thee?' Commentators have simply replied, as does Singleton, 'Such a thing has never happened since the days of St Paul.' St Paul is the obvious answer, but when the person who asks is a Caesar-like figure, St Paul is out of place. Within a Virgilian context, the other choice is Aeneas, to whom was equally given the opportunity to visit the underworld. In fact, Anchises addresses Caesar precisely while showing his son Aeneas his future descendants. The reference strengthens the parallel with Anchises where Cacciaguida addresses Dante, as Anchises did Aeneas when he first sees him: 'del figlio s'accorse' (27). The 'smile' (riso) (34) that Beatrice gives Dante at the end of this exchange would appear to confirm the clever cross-referencing that Dante has just made. Only later, Cacciaguida deigns to lower his language to the level that other mortals can understand: '"l parlar discese/ inver" lo segno del nostro intelletto' [his speech came down towards the mark of our intellect] (44–5).

Cacciaguida's connection with Dante, established through the Anchises-Aeneas parallel, is that he is his great-great-grandfather.

'O fronda mia in che io compiacemmi
    pur aspettando, io fui la tua radice':
    cotal principio, rispondendo, femmi.
Poscia mi disse: 'Quel da cui si dice
    tua cognazione e che cent'anni e piùe
    girato ha il monte in la prima cornice,
mio figlio fu e tuo bisavol fue:
    (*Par.* XV, 88–94)

['O my branch, in whom I rejoiced only expecting you, I was your root.' So he began his answer to me, then said: 'He from whom your house is named and who for a hundred years and more has gone round the mountain on the first terrace was my son and your grandfather's father:]

There is no evidence that Cacciaguida was Dante's ancestor other than these lines.[3] Instead, there is every reason to believe that Cacciaguida is just Dante's fictional ancestor, invented for the sake of drawing a parallel with Caesar and the *Aeneid*. Just as Aeneas meets his father, Anchises, and is shown the souls of the future Romans, so Dante's ancestor, Cacciaguida, provides him with an account of the ancient people of Florence, as they once were. In both cases, the purpose is ironic. In the *Aeneid* what appears to be praise is Virgil's way of condemning greed and violence in (Caesar) Augustus and in the Romans; in Dante, Cacciaguida's account of the early Florentine families is a way to indict the Florentines from their origin.

Another instance of this irony is expressed by Cacciaguida's hope that Dante's fame can abbreviate his son's penance in *Purgatory*:

ben si convien che la lunga fatica
tu li raccorci con l'opere tue.
(*Par.* XV, 95–6)

[it is most fitting that you should shorten his long labour with thy good works.]

The reference, however, serves mainly to situate Dante's ancestor Alighiero in the circle of pride, and to point to what commentators like Singleton have identified as a family failing: pride. 'Superbia,' in fact, is the common trait of Cacciaguida's lineage, from his son, Alighiero, who gave birth to Bello, the father of Bellincione and Geri, who, of course, is already in *Inferno* XXIX as a sower of discord. Geri del Bello, in killing a member of the hated rival family Sacchetti, initiated a feud between the Alighieri and the Sacchetti which did not end until 1342, well after

---

3 See Singleton's commentary to *Paradiso* IV (91); he mentions that R. Davidsohn cites a document where 'there is mention of one Cacciaguida, son of Adam, whom he identifies with Dante's great-great-grandfather.'

Dante's death (see Sapegno). From Bellincione, another Alighiero was born who was Dante's father. Dante, of course, confesses to a similar sin of pride in *Purgatory* XIII (136–8). The irony is that the reference is not only damning for Cacciaguida's son, but it also denounces, by reflection, the father, Cacciaguida. The irony is an instance of what is meant by 'opere tue,' which is Dante's way of placing father and son in the same circle of pride.

There is another reason not to believe that Cacciaguida and Dante are genealogically related. In canto XVII, before Cacciaguida tells Dante of his future exile, there is a disclaimer of any possible paternity through the myth of Apollo and Phaeton. The latter, not satisfied to know that Apollo is his father, wants proof of his paternity and persuades his father to let him drive his chariot, with the result that he comes too close to the sun and falls to his death, 'quei ch'ancor fa li padri ai figli scarsi' [him who still makes fathers wary with their sons] (*Par.* XVII, 3). Phaeton's example is a warning to readers who look for evidence of any relation between Dante and Cacciaguida. Any such relation is impossible to prove, and all attempts will end in failure.

The analogy between Cacciaguida and Julius Caesar is established by the legend, which Dante believed true, that Florence was founded under the auspices of Julius Caesar. The well-known Florentine historian Ferdinand Schevill in his history, *Medieval and Renaissance Florence*, notes how Florence, initially founded as an Etruscan settlement by the people of Fiesole, was destroyed as the result of siding against Sulla in Rome's civil war. When Florence was rebuilt, it became a colony of Rome and was founded, writes Schevill, 'with the conscious purpose on the part of the Latin founders of undoing the havoc caused by the recent devastating civil war':

> In the year 59 BC there was passed during the consulship and under the auspices of Julius Caesar an agrarian law which goes by his name (lex Julia), and which sketched a vigorous program of civic restoration throughout Italy. *The Florentines of the poet Dante's day fondly believed that their city owed its existence to the personal intervention of the great Julius.* That was a legendary exaggeration *born of the desire of the medieval citizenry to be associated not only with conquering Rome but also with Rome's greatest son. However, since the founding undoubtedly took place in consequence of the reconstruction policy championed by Caesar, the medieval tradition was much less removed from the truth* than most of the stories regarding the origins of the

city believed in Dante's time and firmly rooted in Florentine consciousness to this very day.[4] (emphasis mine)

The initial association of Cacciaguida with Julius Caesar re-proposes the history of Florence from its origins, with its destruction as the result of a civil war between Mario and Sulla and its rebirth under Julius Caesar, who engaged in his own civil war with Pompey, his son-in-law, which foreshadows the civil war of Dante's own time between the Guelphs and Ghibellines, those loyal to the Pope and to the Emperor.

Cacciaguida's use of Latin not only clarifies this early association and the nature of his ancestry, what he calls 'io fui la tua radice' [I was your root] (*Par.* XV, 89), but also marks a shift in persona when Cacciaguida's speech changes from Latin to *volgare*. Initially, at the beginning of canto XV, Cacciaguida can be said to double for the figure of Julius Caesar, as Dante's and Florence's Roman *radice*, characterized by his Latin and incomprehensible speech that towers above all others (41–2). Later, when he begins to speak in *volgare*, Cacciaguida is named and becomes Dante's great-great-grandfather. As I have indicated, however, not only is there no hard evidence that a person like Cacciaguida was really Dante's ancestor, but the story of Phaeton and Apollo undermines any possible genealogical relation between him and Dante. In fact, the very notion of 'relazione' [relationship] is questionable in this Heaven of Mars in so far as the 'sweet harmony' (dolce armonia), which it establishes and which seems to permeate the entire dialogue between Dante and Cacciaguida, is as deceitful as it appears harmonious.

This is evident from the story that Cacciaguida recounts of ancient Florence and its golden age. Dante's 'faint' praise of ancient Florence (*Par.* XV, 97ff.) is told by negation, and must be read *not* for what these early citizens did not do, as is stated, but for what *they did*. A series of nine 'non' characterizes Florence and its citizenry as they once were:

Fiorenza dentro dalla cerchia antica,
   ond'ella toglie ancora e terza e nona,
   si stava in pace, sobria e pudica.
Non avea catenella, *non* corona,
   non gonne contigiate, *non* cintura
   che fosse a veder piú che la persona.

---

[4] See Ferdinand Schevill, *Medieval and Renaissance Florence* (New York, Evanston, and London: Harper Torchbooks, 1963; Harper and Row, 1961), 6.

Non faceva, nascendo, ancor paura
    la figlia al padre; ché 'l tempo e la dote
    non fuggíen quinci e quindi la misura.
Non avea case di famiglia vote;
    non v'era giunto ancor Sardanapalo
    a mostrar ciò che 'n camera si pote.
Non era vinto ancora Montemalo
    dal vostro Uccellatoio, che, com'è vinto
    nel montar su, cosí sarà nel calo.
    (*Par.* XV, 97–111; emphasis mine)

[Florence, within her ancient circle from which she still takes tierce and nones, abode in peace, sober and chaste. She had *no* bracelet, *no* tiara, *no* embroidered gowns, *no* girdle that should be seen more than the wearer. *Not* yet did the daughter at her birth put the father in fear, for age and dowry did *not* part from the due measure on the one side and the other. She had *no* houses empty of family, nor had Sardanapalus yet come there to show what could be done in the chamber. *Not* yet did your Uccellatoio surpass Montemario, which, surpassed in its rise, shall be too in its fall.]

These verses imply, on the contrary, that in ancient times Florentine women did go around dressed with lavish adornments to the point that they outshone the person; daughters did make their fathers afraid because of their marrying at a young age with large dowries; the family did decline because of the moral standards of Florentine women. Furthermore, Florentine society had already deteriorated because of its lax and corrupt morals; Florence's prosperity and grandeur was such that it surpassed even Rome, and just as Rome declined so did Florence. Dante's description by negation makes it appear that there was a golden age, that there was a time when Florence and the Florentines were not corrupt and depraved. The truth, however, is that there was never such a time. The passage turns out to be an indictment of what Florence has always been from its origins, and denounces the possibility of an ancient Florence 'sober and chaste' as a lie and a myth.

Cacciaguida's account of his birth is also not very plausible. He wants the reader to believe that he was born at a time when Florence and its citizens were living in a golden age, when we know now that this was not the case. The following lines, which describe the state of Florence when Cacciaguida was born, are, once again, intended to be read ironically:

> A cosí riposato, a cosí bello
> viver di cittadini, a cosí fida
> cittadinanza, a cosí dolce ostello,
> (*Par.* XV, 130–2)

[To a citizen's life so peaceful and so fair, to a community so loyal, to so sweet a dwelling place,]

Dante means, on the contrary, that Cacciaguida was born in a troubled and bleak time, among a citizenry that could not be trusted, and in a city that was really a vipers' nest. In these circumstances, Cacciaguida came into the world! Similarly, the circumstances of his birth described in the line 'Maria mi diè, chiamata in alte grida' [Mary gave me, when called on with loud cries] (*Par.* XV, 133) are not what they appear to be. The line appears to be a simple indication of Cacciaguida's mother giving birth to him among cries of pain. Singleton, in fact, following every commentator, explains the line to mean, 'For Mary invoked by women in the pains of childbirth.' Since not everything is what it seems in this Heaven of Mars, this line is no exception. Though a mother invoking the Virgin at childbirth may very well be one of the intended meanings, the line adds no relevant information to the subject at hand, which is the degraded state in which Cacciaguida was born. The line has other implications which commentators point out but never follow up. The line is usually glossed with *Purgatory* XX (19–22), which describes a similar situation: '"Dolce Maria!"/ dinanzi a noi chiamar cosí nel pianto/ come fa donna che in parturir sia' [I heard one ahead of us crying out in his lament, 'Sweet Mary,' even as a woman does who is in labour]. While these lines at a literal level explain the reference to Mary, they are only part of the meaning. In *Purgatory* XX (19), 'Dolce Maria' is not really the cry of women in childbirth but is spoken by those affected by avarice who voice it as an example of the opposite virtue, which is contempt for wealth and serene acceptance of poverty (see Sapegno's commentary). It is the penitent that cries out 'Dolce Maria,' as if he were a woman giving birth. The cry 'Dolce Maria' alludes to the vices of avarice, greed, and ambition, which are being punished in this terrace of *Purgatory*. If we transpose this indirect meaning to the situation in *Paradiso* XV, it becomes clear how it applies not only to the situation in Florence at the time but also to the circumstances of the birth of Cacciaguida, who can be said to be born under the aegis of 'cupidigia,' greed and ambition; he is himself guilty of these sins, which are punished in *Purgatory* XX, where, as I have already indicated, he really belongs. In this canto, furthermore, it is a question of another 'mala pianta,' Ugo Capeto and the lineage of the Capetingi, who have corrupted Christianity to a point that their tree no longer bears good fruit. By reflection, this is also meant as a commentary on Cacciaguida's family tree.

In *Purgatory* XX, Dante condemns greed and avarice in the figure of the 'lupa,' the she-wolf, first mentioned in *Inferno* I, whose insatiable greed is the cause of most men's evils.

> Maledetta sei tu, *antica lupa*,
>   che più che tutte l'altre bestie hai preda
>   per la tua fame sanza fine cupa!
> (*Purg.* XX, 10–2; emphasis mine)

[Accursed be you, *ancient wolf*, who have more prey than all other beasts, because of your deep and endless hunger!]

Dante's curse is intended for the ancient she-wolf, symbol of Rome and the Roman Empire, the unmistakable 'antica lupa,' whose greed and world ambition, especially in the person of Julius Caesar, is at the root of all the evil that still plagues Florence. Cacciaguida's mother, invoking the Virgin Mary 'in alte grida,' signals, therefore, the pride and ambition that already characterizes him at birth and which makes him another Julius Caesar, another sower of discord, just as his descendants are. For this reason, the other information that Cacciaguida gives about himself, that he was baptized a Christian and took the name Cacciaguida, is similarly suspect.

> *e nell'antico vostro Batisteo*
> *insieme fui cristiano e Cacciaguida.*
> Moronto fu mio frate ed Eliseo:
>   mia donna venne a me di val di Pado;
>   e quindi il sopranome tuo si feo.
> (*Par.* XV, 134–8; emphasis mine)

[*and in your ancient Baptistery I became at once Christian and Cacciaguida.* Moronto was my brother, and Eliseo. My wife came to me from the Po valley, and from her your surname was formed.]

Cacciaguida's claim that he was baptized a Christian in St John's Baptistery requires closer examination. The key word here is 'ancient' (antico), which differentiates the present baptistery of San Giovanni, of Dante's time, from the old and first baptistery, which, as Schevill relates in *Medieval and Renaissance Florence*, probably dates back from 'the period of declining Rome' (242). Although documentary evidence would seem to place the baptistery from the period of the Lombard domination in the seventh century, Schevill also adds that for Dante and Villani, the baptistery was thought to belong to the pagan era, having been built on the ruins of a temple to Mars:

> Dante, Villani, and the local members of the writing tribe down to recent times have voiced the opinion that the baptistery went clear back to the pagan era and that it had originally been a temple of Mars, the god of war. (242)

Even though recent evidence dates the baptistery between the fifth and seventh centuries, and that it 'was erected *ab origine* as a Christian house of worship and that it never had a pagan predecessor'(242), for our reading of the passage we have to accept Dante's version of the facts, which make the circumstances of Cacciaguida's baptism even more poignant. For if we understand the 'antico vostro Batisteo' as a veiled reference to the Temple of Mars, Cacciaguida could be said to have received baptism not in a Christian church but in a pagan temple, the Temple of Mars. The key term is the demonstrative 'vostro' [yours], which indicates by inference (which is how the trope is employed by Dante in the whole canto) that he was born in the place that later became St John's Baptistery. The adjective 'vostro' implies, in fact, that it was *not yet* the present baptistery, and certainly *not* when he was born, otherwise it would have made more sense to say 'ours.' But Cacciaguida can only say 'yours,' and cannot say 'ours,' because where he was born was not yet the baptistery, but the Temple of Mars. In fact, while the reference to Mary and to the baptistery is meant to mislead us into believing that Cacciaguida was a Christian and was baptized in a Christian church, the facts tell otherwise.

The claim that Cacciaguida was given a name and was made a Christian at the same time, 'insieme fui cristiano e Cacciaguida' – the term 'insieme' [together, or 'at once'] as it is translated here – is suspect because it is a truism that at baptism one is given a name and one becomes a Christian at the same time. The mystification resides in the fact that one assumes that the two necessarily follow 'together,' that once Cacciaguida was given his name he also became a Christian. However, since we know now that he was born in what was once the Temple of Mars, when he was given the name Cacciaguida, he could not have been a Christian. He is a Christian by association because he was given a Christian name, Cacciaguida, and because later the Temple of Mars became St John Baptistery, and a Christian church. Similarly, the details of Cacciaguida's relations, of his brothers, 'Moronto fu mio frate ed Eliseo,' and of his wife, 'mia donna venne a me di val di Pado,' and the name of the Alighieri family, 'quindi il sopranome tuo si feo,' lend credence to the fiction of Dante's ancestry and conceal, 'by necessity,' the real nature of Cacciaguida that Dante means to unveil.

The dissimulation which characterizes the figure of Cacciaguida becomes clearer in the final account he gives of how he fought for the Emperor Conrad and died in his service. Since Mars is said to be the heaven of the crusaders for Christ, Cacciaguida has been regarded as someone who 'went forth to die in God's cause' (see Sinclair)[5] at the service of the Emperor Conrad, who knighted him for his services:

> Poi seguitai lo 'mperatore Currado;
>   ed el mi cinse della sua milizia,
>   tanto per bene ovrar li venni in grado
> (*Par.* XV, 139–41)

[Later I followed the Emperor Conrad; and he girded me of his knighthood, so greatly did I win his favour by good service]

He relates that he followed the emperor in fighting the unbelievers in what appears to be a holy crusade, and there he found his death.

> Dietro li andai incontro alla nequizia
>   di quella legge il cui popolo usurpa
>   per colpa de' pastor, vostra giustizia.
> Quivi fu 'io da quella gente turpa
>   disviluppato dal mondo fallace,

---

5 See John D. Sinclair, *Dante's Paradiso*. Italian Text with English translation and comment. Vol. III. (New York: Oxford University Press, 1977) 227.

lo cui amor molt'anime deturpa;
e venni dal martirio a questa pace.'
(*Par.* XV, 142–8)

[I followed him against the iniquity of that law whose people, by fault of the shepherds, usurp your right. There I was set free by that foul people from the entanglements of the deceitful world, the love of which corrupts many souls, and came from martyrdom to this peace.']

From what has been said so far, however, there are very good reasons to doubt this version of events. We know that Conrad III took part in the second Crusade (1147– 1149), but we also know that he never came to Italy, so Cacciaguida could not have followed him to the Holy Land. Perhaps the clue to what is really going on are in Cacciaguida's words, which recall those attributed to Boethius in *Paradiso* X:

Per vedere ogni ben dentro vi gode
  l'anima santa *che 'l mondo fallace*
  fa manifesto a chi di lei ben ode:
lo corpo ond'ella fu cacciata giace
  giuso in Centauro; ed essa da martiro
  e da essilio venne a questa pace.
  (*Par.* X, 124–9; emphasis mine)

[Within it the holy soul rejoices in the vision of all the good *who makes plain the world's deceitfulness to one who hears him rightly*; the body from which he was driven lives below in Centauro, and he came from martyrdom and exile to this peace.]

The two passages are linked by a similarity in rhyme scheme: 'fallace,' 'giace,' and 'pace,' although in *Paradiso* XV the canto ends before the rhyme in 'giace.' As commentators like Sinclair point out, the similarity between the two passages is both 'intentional and significant,' and he explains the meaning as follows: 'Boethius exposed the world's deceitfulness to the world, and he served God well; Cacciaguida fought and gave his life against it, and he served God better – that was his "higher blessedness."' (see Sinclair's commentary on *Paradiso* XV, 227). For Sinclair, Cacciaguida is even worthier than Boethius in his service to God! But the actual differences between the two quotations tell a different story. One essential difference is that Cacciaguida is slain by the deceitful world from which he comes ('disviluppato dal mondo fallace'), while Boethius denounced this deceitful world ('che 'l mondo fallace fa manifesto a chi di lei ben ode'). It is the latter part of the line, 'a chi di lei ben ode,' which intimates that Boethius' denunciation of the 'mondo fallace' is not apparent to everyone, just as deceit never is, but must be detected by those who know how to listen ('a chi ben ode'). What we ought to listen to, in our case, is the difference between the two passages that denounce Cacciaguida's deceit. The 'amor' which 'molt'anime deturpa' (for which Cacciaguida met his death) is not the love of the wrong god, but greed, ambition, and pride, which Dante has identified with the 'lupa' [she-wolf].

Cacciaguida's deceit can be read in the very same lines that describe his role as a crusader for Christ, and which point to his leading role at the service of the Emperor against the 'iniquities' of a papacy that challenged and usurped imperial power. Cacciaguida died fighting for the Emperor but not in the Holy Land against the Saracens. The 'gente turpa' are rather those who sided with the pope ('per colpa de' pastor'), whose wicked laws ('nequizia/di quella legge') usurped the land belonging to the emperor. To shed light on this hidden aspect of Cacciaguida's past we must pass to the next canto, where the real version of the good people of ancient Florence is made clear in the other reference to the baptistery in *Paradiso* XVI, when Dante asks him who his ancestors are and who were Florence's worthiest citizens of his time.

> Ditemi dunque, cara mia primizia,
>   quai fuor li vostri antichi, e quai fuor li anni
>   che si segnaro in vostra puerizia:
> ditemi *dell'ovil di San Giovanni*
>   *quanto era allora*, e che eran le genti
>   tra esse degne di più alti scanni.'
> (Par. XVI, 22–7; emphasis mine)

[Tell me then, dear stock from which I spring, what was your ancestry and what were the years that were reckoned in your boyhood. Tell me of the sheepfold of St John, how it was then, and who were the folk within it worthy of the highest seats.']

Cacciaguida's reply is rather brief and dismissive:

> Li antichi miei e io nacqui nel loco
>   dove si truova pria l'ultimo sesto
>   da quel che corre il vostro annual giuoco.
> Basti de' miei maggiori udirne questo:
>   chi ei si fosser e onde venner quivi,
>   *piú è tacer che ragionare onesto.*
>   (*Par.* XVI, 40–5; emphasis mine)

[My ancestors and I were born at the place where the furthest ward is reached by the runner in your yearly games. Let it suffice you to hear this much of my forebears as to who they were and whence they came *it is more honest to be silent than to speak.*]

Commentators have interpreted Cacciaguida's reticence as 'the pride of a great gentleman,' and that 'probably what is told us here is all that Dante knew of his forebears' (see Sinclair, 239). However, the contrary is the case because Cacciaguida would rather not discuss the good Christians, who like him were baptized in the 'ovil di San Giovanni.' He would rather be silent than speak the truth and expose his ancestors, and himself, for the corrupt people they were. In fact, we are not dealing with a sheepfold of good Christians, as it may appear at first, but with a den of wolves.

The truth is revealed in the lines that follow, except that Cacciaguida's account appears to refer to a later period, when Florence has become a corrupt state and is in decline as a result of ethnic mixing that took place between the pure ancient populace of Florence and the impure people that came from the countryside.

> Tutti color ch'a quel tempo eran ivi
>   da poter arme tra Marte e 'l Batista,
>   eran il quinto di quel ch'or son vivi.
> *Ma la cittadinanza, ch'è or mista*
>   di Campi, di Certaldo e di Fegghine,
>   pura vedíesi nell'ultimo artista.
>   (*Par.* XVI, 46–51; emphasis mine)

[All those able to bear arms who at the time were there, between Mars and the Baptist, were fifth of the number now living. *But the citizenship, which is now mixed* with Campi and Certaldo and Figline, was pure down to the humblest artisan.]

It is clear, however, from these lines that the period referred to is an earlier one, which goes from 'Marte' to 'Batista.' The reference, which has always been interpreted as indicating a spatial difference between the Baptistery and the statue of Mars on Ponte Vecchio, indicates the time period between the original temple of Mars and when it became St John's Baptistry, which was erected on its foundations. It is to this period that Dante refers when the Florentines, which Cacciaguida now passes in review, lived.

The group of Florentines that Cacciaguida introduces are not from the city but from the neighboring towns, and he does not hide his dislike and disdain for them whom he blames for corrupting the morals and pure ways of life of ancient Florence.

> Oh quanto fora meglio esser vicine
>   quelli genti ch'io dico, e al Galluzzo
>   e a Trespiano aver vostro confine,
> che averle dentro e sostener lo puzzo
>   del villan d'Aguglion, di quel da Signa
>   che già per barattare ha l'occhio aguzzo!
>   (*Par.* XVI, 52–7)

[Ah, how much better it would be that those people of whom I speak were neighbours, and to have your boundary at Galluzzo and at Trespiano, than to have them within and to endure the stench of the boor from Aguglione, and from Signa, who already has his eye sharp for jobbery!]

Cacciaguida blames the neighboring towns and the expansion of communal jurisdictions into the city for Florence's decline, for corrupting the morals and honest habits of its citizens, whereas the good ancient people of Florence seem to be exempt of all blame.

> Sempre la confusion delle persone
>   principio fu del mal della cittade,
>   come del vostro il cibo che s'appone.
>   (*Par.* XVI, 67–9)

[The confusion of people was ever the beginning of harm to the city, as to you the food which is loaded on is to the body.]

The reason behind this 'confusion,' which was the beginning of the fall of the city of Florence, seems to be papal hostility against the emperor. If the pope had not interfered with the temporal power of the emperor (Caesar), and had not been hostile to him, as a stepmother (noverca), by abandoning the right and natural way that had been divinely assigned to each of sharing the temporal and the spiritual powers between Church and Empire, civil institutions would not have declined and become corrupt, and the area around Florence would not have been destabilized, and there would not have been reason for feuds like Montemurlo and other villages to move into Florence.

> Se la gente ch'al mondo piú traligna
>   non fosse stata a Cesare noverca,
>   ma come madre a suo figlio benigna
> [...]
> saríesi Montemurlo ancor de' Conti
> sarìeno i Cerchi nel piovier d'Acone,
> e forse in Valdigrieve i Buondelmonti.
> (*Par.* XVI, 58–60, 64–6)

[If the people that of all the world are most degenerate had not been a stepmother to Caesar, but kind like a mother to her son [...] Montemurlo would still belong to the Counts, the Cerchi would be in the Acone parish, and the Buondelmonti perhaps in Valdigreve.]

On close analysis, however, the contrary seems to be the case. The people from the villages were, in fact, simple people lacking the manners and social mores of the city folk, who, on the other hand, were people of few scruples, always ready to make a deal and seize an opportunity to make a profit. Cacciaguida's account, in fact, is contradicted by what is stated in line 61, which I have omitted intentionally from the previous quotation. This line is the beam of light, if you will, that shows the hidden story behind an otherwise perfect façade:

> *tal fatto è fiorentino e cambia e merca,*
>   che si sarebbe volto a Simifonti,

là dove andava l'avolo alla cerca
(*Par.* XVI, 61–3; emphasis mine)

[*this fact is Florentine who changes and trades*, who would have lived in Semifonte, where his grandfather went begging]

The line states that money-changing, or usury, and trading were already a Florentine trait, whereas the people from the neighboring village were simple folk, engaged in simple trade, or were even beggars (andava l'avolo alla cerca). These people would have continued to live in this manner had they not been forced to move to Florence. It is in Florence and from the Florentines that they learned the art of marketing and money lending, 'e cambia e merca.' From them they learned greed and how to cheat, because these are Florentine qualities and specialties: 'tal fatto è fiorentino.' Rather than being responsible for corrupting the Florentines, the people from the surrounding villages were in fact corrupted by those who had already developed their miserly arts, which brought about their downfall long before they were joined by these rural folks. As we know from historical accounts,[6] they were annexed to Florence because of the city's expansionist politics, and were forced to move to the city and adopt Florentine customs and lifestyle. The blame for Florence's ills, therefore, rests squarely on the Florentines themselves, and on their territorial ambition and greed.

If the pope, or the Guelph ruling party, were behind this expansionist drive, this is only half the equation. What is left unmentioned and implied is the role of the Emperor and the men of arms who were at his service, such as Cacciaguida. In fact, the allusion to Caesar, 'non fosse stata a Cesare noverca' [had not been a stepmother to Caesar] (*Par.* XVI, 59), is not only a reference to the Emperor, as I have indicated, but also an indirect reference to Cacciaguida, who is associated with Julius Caesar, and implicates him as having had a similar role in Florence's civil war between the Florentines and the surrounding communes. This association explains the pivotal role that Cacciaguida had in it, for which he boasts of having been made a knight by the Emperor. The Holy War Cacciaguida was conducting on behalf of the Emperor, therefore, was not against the Saracens in the Holy Land, as it appears at first, but against the Guelphs, the 'gente turpa' who sided with the pope in Florence's civil war.

---

6 See note 4.

The Heaven of Mars is also the Heaven of Florence and the Cross made up of blessed souls already anticipates the destruction of Florence. The story that Cacciaguida tells us, which parallels Anchises' enumeration of Aeneas' progeny in the *Aeneid*, is only apparently an encomium. It is the story of Florence's decline and degeneration, and eventual destruction, because of the civil wars that raged in Florence from its origins. This decline, however, was not brought about by an influx of people from neighboring villages who corrupted the virtue and morals of the ancient Florentines, and marked an end to Florence's golden age. The opposite is the case. Dante tells us that Florence from its origins has been implicated in civil wars, and that the city had always been a battleground long before the Guelphs and the Ghibellines perpetuated the conflict. This is made clear, indirectly, in the story that the apparently pious and loving Florentine families tell of cities like Troy, Fiesole, and Rome:

> l'altra, traendo alla rocca la chioma,
>   favoleggiava con la sua famiglia
>   *de' Troiani, di Fiesole e di Roma.*
> (*Par.* XV, 124–6; emphasis mine)

[another, drawing the tresses from the distaff, would tell among her family tales *of Trojans, Fiesole and Rome.*]

In the opinion of Singleton, 'The telling of such "founding" tales attests essentially to the "piety" (in the Latin sense of *pietas*) of the good people of old Florence, as Dante would have it' (Singleton's commentary). These lines, however, conceal a more grim reality, which is alluded to in the surprising presence of Fiesole between Troy and Rome. While Troy and Rome are linked, as in Virgil's *Aeneid*, through Aeneas, whose descendants founded Rome, there is no apparent link with Fiesole. The presence of Fiesole functions similarly to the disruptive presence of Turnus between Euryalus and Nisus in *Inferno* I (108): 'Eurialo e Turno e Niso di ferute' [Euryalus and Turnus and Nisus [died] of their wounds].[7] It signals that at the origins of Florence there was the destruction of Fiesole by the Romans as a result of the civil war between Marius and Sulla. But Fiesole had an even greater impact on Florence

---

7 See my discussion of the importance of Turnus' presence amongst the other warriors in chapter 3 of *Reading Dante Reading*.

because the first people to inhabit the city were in large part from Fiesole, and a small part was made up of Roman families from the legions that had occupied the area. As the chronicler Villani reports, and as Dante, through Brunetto Latini in *Inferno* XV, seems to believe, the people from Fiesole were coarse and warmongers, while the Romans were noble and virtuous (38): 'The Florentines are always in disagreement and at war among themselves. Nor need that cause amazement, since they descend from two opposed, inimical, and very different peoples – namely, the noble and virtuous Romans and the crude, war-embittered Fiesolans' (Villani I, 38; cited by Singleton in his commentary to *Inf*. XV, 62). This view is espoused in Dante's encounter with Brunetto Latini in the corresponding canto, *Inferno* XV:

> Ma quello ingrato popolo maligno
>   che discese di Fiesole ab antico,
>   e tiene ancor del monte e del macigno,
> ti si si farà per tuo ben far, nemico:

and later:

> Vecchia fama li chiama orbi;
>   gent'è avara, invidiosa e superba:
>   dai lor costumi fa che tu ti forbi
>   [...]
> Faccian le bestie fiesolane strame
>   di lor medesme, e non tocchin la pianta,
>   s'alcuna surge ancora in lor letame
> *in cui riviva la sementa santa*
>   *di que' Roman che vi rimaser quando*
>   *fu fatto il nido di malizia tanta.*
> (*Inf*. XV, 61–4, 67–9, 73–8; my emphasis)

[But that thankless, malignant people, who of old came down from Fiesole, and still smacks of the mountain and the rock, will make themselves an enemy to you because of your good deeds [...] Old world fame calls them blind; it is a people avaricious, envious and proud: look that you cleanse yourself of their customs [...] Let the Fiesolan beasts make fodder of themselves, and not touch the plant (if any spring yet upon their dungheap) in which survives the holy seed of those Romans who remained there when it became the nest of so much wickedness.]

In this account, Dante seems to be squarely on the side of the noble Romans and their 'sementa santa' [holy seed] (76), as he appears to be in *Paradiso* XV when he takes pride in being a descendant of Cacciaguida and Caesar. This is certainly true of the Dante of the *Convivio*, but not of the *Commedia*, as is evident from his critique of Virgil in *Inferno* I, and in *Paradiso* XV. The pro-Roman sentiments voiced here are those of Brunetto Latini, who, as Singleton points out in his commentary, can be found in his *Tresor*. Dante is being very much ironic here, as in the rest of the canto, but he is not ironic with respect to the Florentine-Fiesolani. As Singleton points out, the title of the poem, as it appears in manuscripts, makes this very clear: 'Incipit Comedia Dantis Alighierii florentini natione, non moribus' [Here begins the Comedy of Dante Alighieri, a Florentine by birth but not by character] (see Singleton's commentary to *Inf.* XV, 69).

The disruptive presence of Fiesole between Troy and Rome denounces, first of all, the Virgilian version of a continuity between Troy and Rome – willed by the gods, to found Rome as a new Troy – as just a fairy tale. 'l'altra [...] favoleggiava con la sua famiglia/ d'i Troiani, di Fiesole e di Roma' [Another [...] told her household the tale of the Trojans, Fiesole and Rome] (*Par.* XV, 124–6). The presence of Fiesole undermines the Virgilian fairy tale of noble and virtuous Romans and reminds us of the tragic reality of civil wars, of the destruction of cities, and the passing of kings, which is the only continuity that can be established between Troy and Rome. It is a reminder that the origins of Florence's evils are in the destruction of Fiesole, and that Florence inherited not just its inhabitants but its fate. This is the real origin of Florence's civil war and not the feud between the Guelphs and Ghibellines, which is conveniently blamed on Buondelmonti's refusal to marry an Amidei. Buondelmonti was only the 'convenient' sacrificial victim for the ills that began with the foundation of Florence.

> Ma *conveníesi* a quella pietra scema
>   che guarda 'l ponte che Fiorenza fesse
> vittima nella sua pace postrema.
>   (*Par.* XVI, 145–7; emphasis mine)

[But it was *convenient* to Florence, in her last days of peace, to offer a victim to that mutilated stone that guards the bridge.]

Heaven of Mars: Music   103

Dante's history of Florence's civil war, told in reverse ('a ritroso') to get to its 'real' causes, is allegorized in a final image of a white lily, the symbol of Florence, which turns red as it is dragged backwards on the ground with a spear:

> Con queste genti vid'io glorioso
>   e giusto il popol suo, tanto che 'l giglio
>   non era ad asta mai posto *a ritroso*,
> nè per division fatto vermiglio.
>   (*Par.* XVI, 151–4).

[With these I saw her people so glorious and so just that the lily had never been *reversed* on the spear, nor dissension changed to red.]

This is the tragic history of Florence, as told by Dante, in the spirit of Lucan.

***

To return to Cacciaguida's involvement in Florence's civil wars, Dante provides a clue, as usual in this Heaven of Mars, indirectly, through the juxtaposition of two passages that echo each other, just as we saw earlier for the Boethius passage in *Paradiso* X, where one passage stands for the ray of sun that sheds light on the obscurity of the other. The first passage is from canto XVI (58–63), where Cacciaguida relates the Florentines' betrayal of the Emperor:

> Se la gente ch'al mondo più traligna
>   non fosse stata a Cesare *noverca*,
>   ma come madre a suo figlio benigna,
> tal fatto è fiorentino e cambia e *merca*,
>   che si sarebbe volto a Simifonti,
>   là dove andava l'avolo alla *cerca*;
>   (*Par.* XVI, 58–63; emphasis mine)

[If the folk who are the most degenerate in the world had not been a *stepmother* to Caesar, but, like a mother, benignant to her son, this fact is Florentine, and change and trade, who would have turned to Semifonti, where the ancient went begging;]

104   The Poetics of Dante's *Paradiso*

Cacciaguida speculates what would have happened if popes and the Roman curia had respected the rights of the Emperor and had not contrasted him. The passage through the rhyme scheme: noverca, cerca, merca, alludes to a passage in *Paradiso* XVII where it is question of another 'noverca' and of a similar rhyme scheme.

> Qual si partío Ippolito d'Atene
>   per la spietata e *perfida noverca*
>   tal di Fiorenza partir ti convene.
> Questo si vuole e questo già si *cerca*,
>   e tosto verrà fatto a chi ciò pensa
>   là dove Cristo tutto dì si *merca*.
>   (*Par.* XVII, 46–51; emphasis mine)

> [As Hippolytus was driven from Athens on account of his cruel and perfidious *stepmother*, so must you be driven from Florence. So it is willed, so already *plotted*, and so shall be accomplished soon by him who ponders upon it in the place where every day Christ is *bought and sold*.]

The passage recounts how Hippolytus was banished by his father, Theseus, because of Phedra's false accusations that he had attempted to dishonour her. In appearance, the Ovidian story serves to describe Dante's banishment and exile from Florence for unjust cause, but the similarity in rhyme scheme with the previous passage indicates that there is more at stake in these verses.

To begin with the passage from *Paradiso* XVI, the usual reading of 'la gente ch'al mondo più traligna' [the folk who are the most degenerate in the world] (*Par.* XVI. 58), as referring to popes and the Roman curia, is misleading. Read together with the Hippolytus' passage, and in terms of Cacciaguida's role in the expansionist role of the Florence of that period, it becomes clear that 'la gente ch'al mondo più traligna' are the folks living outside Florence who do not wish to bow to Florence's will. If these communities and towns had been more amenable to Caesar and to his expansionist policies, and treated Florence as a mother and not as a stepmother (which is how the folks from these surrounding communities must have felt about Florence and the Florentines), there would have been no civil war and their towns would not have been destroyed. More specifically, Caesar would not have turned against Semifonte, a fortress in the Val d'Elsa which was destroyed by Florence after four years of siege. But as Singleton (commentary to lines 62–3) points out, these lines are not comprehensible: 'The point of Cacciaguida's allusion, which appears to be some special circumstance, is not now understood,' However, in the context we have provided, the 'special circumstances' can be said to be the siege and destruction of Semifonte, in which we can assume that Cacciaguida took part, and, perhaps, found his death. In fact, if the passage is read by omitting line 61, as I have suggested previously, Cacciaguida's words are clear.

> Se la gente ch'al mondo più traligna
>   non fosse stata a Cesare *noverca*,
>   ma come madre a suo figlio benigna,
> (tal fatto è fiorentino e cambia e *merca*,)
>   che si sarebbe volto a Simifonti,
>   là dove andava l'avolo alla *cerca*;
> (*Par.* XVI, 58–63; emphasis mine)

What Cacciaguida is saying is that if the country folks had looked to Florence as a mother and not as a stepmother, Caesar would not have besieged and destroyed Semifonte. Line 61 makes the passage incomprehensible because Dante meant to denounce the action as a Florentine act of aggression and not the other way around, as Cacciaguida's account seems to state. Furthermore, the lines that indicate the defeat of Semifonte are really an indictment of the Florentines and of Cacciaguida:

> Oh quali io vidi quei che son disfatti
>   per lor superbia!
> (*Par.* XVI, 109–10)

[Oh how many I have seen who were undone by their pride!]

As I indicated, 'the amor' that 'molt'anime deturpa' (*Par.* XV, 147–8) is greed and ambition, and it applies equally to the Florentines and to Cacciaguida. If we transpose this meaning to the Hippolytus passage in *Paradiso* XVII, which prophesies Dante's exile (an event which has already occurred at the time of writing this canto), the blame that will fall on those responsible for Dante's exile will fall ironically on Cacciaguida himself.

106   The Poetics of Dante's *Paradiso*

> Questo si vuole e questo già si *cerca*,
>   e tosto verrà fatto a chi ciò pensa
> là dove Cristo tutto dì si *merca*.
> (*Par.* XVII, 49–51)

[So it is willed, so already *plotted*, and so shall be accomplished soon by him who ponders upon it in the place where every day Christ is *bought and sold*.]

The place referred to here is usually thought to be the Roman curia, but the place meant by Dante is Florence where the Guelphs, who are allies of the pope, conduct their business to their sole advantage.

The just punishment for the Florentines, and for Cacciaguida, will not be late in arriving: 'ma la vendetta/ fia testimonio al ver che la dispensa' [but vengeance shall bear witness to the truth which dispenses it] *(Par.* XVII, 53–4). In fact, it has already arrived with these cantos of the Heaven of Mars. Ironically, Cacciaguida's lines that refer to Dante's objective in the *Paradiso* as DXV are meant, first of all, for Cacciaguida himself.

> indi rispuose: Coscienza fusca
>   o della propria o dell'altrui vergogna
> pur sentirà la tua parola brusca.
> Ma nondimen, *rimossa ogni menzogna*,
>   tutta tua vision fa manifesta;
> e lascia pur grattar dov'è la rogna.
> Chè se la voce tua sarà molesta
>   nel primo gusto, *vital nutrimento
> lascerà poi,* quando sarà digesta.
> (*Par.* XVII, 124–32; emphasis mine)

[Then replied: Conscience dark with its own or another's shame will indeed feel your words to be harsh; but none the less *removed every falsehood* make plain all your vision – and let them scratch where they itch. For if your voice is grievous at first taste, afterwards *it will leave vital nourishmen* when it is digested.]

Dante's vision, as well as the punishment that his harsh words (parola brusca) dole out, is predicated on the possibility of *removing* the lie which conceals the evil and fraudulent actions, not only of the sinners in *Inferno* and *Purgatory* but also of the 'pious' souls in *Paradiso*. The act of removing every falsehood also echoes the mandate of the Veltro, whose aim is to pursue the she-wolf (lupa), the symbol of greed, pride, and ambition, and to denounce its deceit wherever it finds it, even in Paradise. In the Heaven of Mars, Dante reiterates the benefits that the reader will receive from these insights, which, like those of the Veltro, will not teach the reader how to become wealthy or successful (greedy, in other words), but will teach him how to become wiser, more loving, and more virtuous. While Dante's poetic word might seem distasteful (molesta) to some at first, because it indicts people apparently beyond reproach, like Cacciaguida, it will provide 'vital nutrimento' (*Par.* XVII, 131) in the knowledge of the deceit which is concealed behind a beautiful appearance.

At the representational level, the objectives of the DXV in *Paradiso* are fulfilled, as we have seen, by means of allegory and irony. In either case, what is at stake is the didactic character of Dante's poetry, and that poetry is knowledge, if only one takes the time to read it and understand it. Cacciaguida makes this point when he suggests that the characters presented in the poem have been selected because of their importance, 'l'anime che son di fama note' [only souls who are known by fame] (*Par.* XVII, 138), since readers are not interested in the fate of ordinary people: 'che l'animo di quel ch'ode, non posa/né ferma fede per essemplo ch'aia/ la sua radice incognita ed ascosa, nè per altro argomento che non paia' [because the mind of the listener will not pay attention or believe an example whose roots are unknown or hidden, or for reasons that are not manifest] (139–42). These lines reiterate the allegorical nature of the poem, since what is at stake is not a judgment of the character per se, that is, of Virgil, Paolo and Francesca, Ulysses, Brunetto Latini, Cacciaguida, but of what they stand for. Dante chooses these important figures to catch the interest of the reader, yet his aim is not directed at them personally, but to what they represent allegorically. These characters are only poetic fictions or allegories that have to be read for the meaning they conceal and for the vital understanding they provide. But this meaning has to be deciphered because it is never apparent at first: 'né per altro argomento che non paia.' The irony is clear. Readers do not like to figure out the sense of a poem, as it happened for the *canzoni* of the *Convivio*, but if the reader wishes to acquire the wisdom promised by the poem, he or she will have to read 'obliquely' between the lines to go to the root ('radice') of Dante's argument, which is never apparent at first. Only when we readjust our sight, 'rinovando vista' *(Par.* XIV, 113), through a cross-reading similar to a light that shines through a dark room, are we able to see through Cacciaguida's deceit and to denounce his shady past.

6 Heaven of Jupiter: Geometry (XVIII–XX)

E lo cielo di Giove si può comparare a la Geometria per due proprietadi: l'una si è che muove tra due cieli repugnanti a la sua buona temperanza, sì come quello di Marte e quello di Saturno; onde Tolomeo dice, ne lo allegato libro, che Giove è stella di temperata complessione, in mezzo della freddura di Saturno e de lo calore di Marte; l'altra si è che intra tutte le stelle bianca si mostra quasi argentata. E queste cose sono ne la scienza de la Geometria. La Geometria si muove intra due repugnanti a essa, sì come lo punto e lo cerchio – e dico "cerchio" largamente ogni ritondo, o corpo o superficie – ché, sì come dice Euclide, lo punto è principio di quella, e, secondo che dice, lo cerchio è perfettissima figura in quella, che conviene però avere ragione di fine. Sì che tra 'l punto e lo cerchio sì come tra principio e fine si muove la Geometria, e questi due a la sua certezza repugnano; ché lo punto per la sua indivisibilitade è immensurabile, e lo cerchio per lo suo arco è impossibile a quadrare perfettamente, e però è impossibile a misurare a punto. E ancora: la Geometria è bianchissima, in quanto è sanza macula d'errore e certissima per sé e per la sua ancella, che si chiama Perspettiva. (*Conv.* II, xiii, 25–8)

[The heaven of Jupiter may be compared to Geometry on account of two properties: the first is that it moves between two heavens antithetical to its admirable temperateness, those of Mars and Saturn; so Ptolemy says, in the work cited, that Jupiter is a star of temperate quality, midway between the cold of Saturn and the heat of Mars. The second property is that it alone among the stars is white in appearance, as if covered in silver. These features are also found in the science of Geometry. Geometry moves between two things antithetical to it, the point and the circle: as Euclid says, the point is the primary element in Geometry, and, as he also indicates, the circle is its most perfect figure, and must, therefore, be considered its end. So Geometry moves between the point and the circle as between its beginning and its end; and both of these are antithetical to the certainty characteristic of this science, for the point cannot be measured at all, since it cannot be divided, and the circle cannot be measured precisely, since, being curved, it cannot be perfectly squared. Furthermore geometry is of the purest white in that it is free of any taint of error, and utterly certain both in itself and its ancillary science, called Perspective.]

The Heaven of Jupiter accounts for three more cantos. In the first we are shown a superb geometric display directed by God the Supreme Geometer, who, in this fashion, introduces the theme of Monarchy, when the souls form an M and then an Eagle; in the second canto we have the history of Monarchy narrated by the Eagle; and in the third we have an excursus of those rulers who were considered just. But not everything is perfect even in the temperate Heaven of Jupiter, since it suffers from the influences of Mars and Saturn, which are hot and cold, respectively. Similarly, Geometry, which in itself is 'without error' (senza macula d'errore) and very certain (certissima), because it moves between the point that cannot be measured (immensurabile) and the circle that cannot be perfectly squared (impossibile a quadrare perfettamente), is also uncertain because both the point and the circle cannot be measured. These adverse influences undermine the perfect temperate Heaven of Jupiter and the design of Geometry.

The beginning of canto XVIII, as usual, sets the tone to the main theme of the cantos, which is temperance, with reference to the prophecy that Dante has just received from Cacciaguida: 'e io gustava/lo mio, temprando col dolce l'acerbo' [and I was tasting mine, tempering the bitter with the sweet] (*Par.* XVIII, 2–3). Just as Dante tempers the bad news of his exile with the good news of the poem he will write, so the Heaven of Jupiter, 'lo candor della temprata stella' [the candor of the temperate star] (68), tempers the two opposite tendencies of Mars' extreme heat and Saturn's extreme cold.

The highlight of the canto are the blessed souls who sing the first line of Wisdom: DILIGITE IUSTITIAM QUI IUDICATIS TERRAM, later displayed in written form:

> sì dentro ai lumi sante creature
>   volitando cantavano, e faciensi
>   or D, or I, or L in sue figure.

Prima, cantando, a sua nota moviensi;
   poi, diventando l'un di questi segni,
   un poco s'arrestavano e taciensi.
   (*Par.* XVIII, 76–81)

[so within the lights holy creatures were singing as they flew and made themselves, in the figures they formed, now D, now I, now L. First, singing, they moved to their own notes; then, becoming one of these shapes, they paused for a little and were silent.]

The souls order themselves to form the letter M, symbol of Monarchy, the embodiment of Justice; and from the letter M, these lights go on to form the head and neck of the Imperial Eagle, 'la testa e 'collo d'un'aguglia vidi' [I saw the head and neck of an eagle] (107). These lights are obeying the grand design of God, who is the Great Geometer Himself, 'Quei che dipinge lí, non ha chi 'l guidi' [He that designs there has none to guide Him] (109). But even in this temperate heaven the unexpected occurs! It seems that a rebel group of Guelphs, reluctant to give up their standard, instead of an Eagle wants to form a Florentine Lily, but then slowly, and reluctantly (con poco moto), they move quickly to join the others to form the Imperial Eagle.

L'altra beatitudo, che contenta
   pareva prima d'ingigliarsi all'emme,
   con poco moto seguitò la 'mprenta.
   (*Par.* XVIII, 112–14; emphasis mine)

[The rest of the blessed spirits, which *seemed at first content to form a lily* on the M, *in slow motion*, followed out the design.]

This reading suggested by Parodi has always been discarded, since, as Sapegno points out, it hardly seems to be coherent with the whole episode ('non sembra che possa inserirsi in maniera coerente nell'invenzione generale'). But this is precisely the point; it does not fit because the Guelphs would like to boycott the grand design of the Monarchy, which is being displayed and of which they are forced to be a part, but cannot, of course. In accordance with what Dante writes about the Heaven of Jupiter, this sense of contrariness, 'repugnare,' is to be expected, because the apparent boycott by the Guelph souls is an example of influence from Mars. The blessed souls, however, have no choice but to follow the divine design; thus their recalcitrance and slowness in adhering to the divine plan, and their attempt to form a lily instead of an eagle is an interesting example of rebellion to the divine plan, as well as a subtle use of irony on Dante's part!

That this is not a casual, unintended incident is shown by the rest of canto XVIII, which discusses, precisely, those who have been misled by the bad example provided by popes and the Roman curia: 'tutti sviati dietro al malo essemplo!' [all led astray by ill example] (*Par.* XVIII, 126). Dante mentions Pope John XXII, who gains wealth by easily giving interdicts and excommunications, which he cancels in exchange for monetary compensation: 'che sol per cancellare scrivi' [you write only to cancel] (130). This pope turned his back on the apostles Peter and Paul to become a devotee of John the Baptist, alluding to the Florin, the Florentine coin that bears his image. Both the case of the Guelph souls and of Pope John XXII are mirror examples of what in this canto is called the smoke that tarnishes your light: 'il fummo che 'l tuo raggio vizia' [the smoke that dims thy beam] (120), namely, the corruption and injustice that tarnished God's image both on earth and in this heaven.

In canto XIX, the Eagle, which is a composite of all the souls, stands for the unity of the one and the many, speaking for everyone but in a single voice, just as the Monarch does, *e pluribus unum*, 'ch'io vidi e anche udi' parlar lo rostro/e sonar nella voce e "io" e "mio,"/quand'era nel concetto"noi" e "nostro"' [For I saw and I heard the beak talk and utter with its voice "I and mine" when its meaning was we and ours (*Par.* XIX, 10–12)]. The story of the Eagle, however, reflects very much the division which characterizes justice on earth. The Eagle stands as the symbol of the just and merciful prince who is not overcome by desire for worldly glory and possessions, but its example is lost on the princes of the earth who do not follow its model (la storia). They ignore that the only worthwhile glory is the greater glory of God, and seek only glory for themselves, and are cruel and corrupt.

> E cominció: 'Per esser giusto e pio
> son io qui essaltato a *quella gloria*
> *che non si lascia vincere a disio*;
> e in terra lasciai la mia memoria
> sì fatta, che le genti *lí malvage*
> commendan lei, ma non seguon la storia.'
> (*Par.* XIX, 13–9; emphasis mine)

[And it began: 'For being just and merciful I am here exalted *to that glory which desire cannot surpass*, and on earth I left such a memory that *the wicked people there commend it but do not continue its story.*']

The story of the Eagle is interrupted by Dante's doubt and by the Eagle's answer as to God's inscrutability, and whether those who have never known the word of God will be saved. The Eagle's demonstration of those that God has saved takes up canto XX. Tucked at the end of canto XIX, instead, is the enumeration of all those wicked princes that never followed the Eagle's example *(Par. XIX, 115–48)*.

Dante mentions the open Book of Justice (volume aperto) (114) where one can read all the abuses (dispregi) of the wicked kings. Dante organizes them according to the acrostic LVE, meaning 'plague,' to stress that the wicked princes are the plague of humanity and Christianity: (L) Emperor Albert of Austria, who will destroy Bohemia and take it away from his brother-in-law Wenceslaus; (L) Philip the Fair, who, in order to get money after the battle of Courtrai, coined false money causing misery to his people; (L) Edward II, the king of England, and Robert Bruce, the King of Scotland, whose thirst for power blinds them with rage against one another; (V) The life of lust and debauchery of Ferdinand IV of Castile and Wenceslaus IV, king of Bohemia, who never knew valor on the battlefield or even looked for it; (V) Charles II of Naples, titular king of Jerusalem, whose good works are recorded in the book with the number 1, and his wickedness with M, 1000; (V) Frederick of Aragon, king of Sicily, is mentioned for his miserliness and cowardice, 'avarizia e la viltate,' and his misdeeds will be recorded in shorthand so that one can fit all of his misdeeds into a short space; (E) James king of Majorca and Minorca, and James II of Aragon, king of Sicily, the uncle and the brother of Frederick, respectively, both of whom have dishonoured their lineage with their base and vile actions; (E) Dionysius, king of Portugal, and Haakon VII, king of Norway, are mentioned, with Stephen Urosh II, king of Serbia, who counterfeited the Venetian ducat. In the final invective, the Eagle mentions the throne of Hungary and Navarre, hoping they will not let themselves be annexed by the French usurpers. The lamentations and the rebukes of the people of Cyprus against their dissolute king Henry II of Lusignan should serve them as a warning! In other words, the story of the Monarchy as told by the Eagle is a story of corruption, debauchery, and vile and base actions. Justice is nowhere to be found!

The third disruption occurs in canto XX as a result of the Eagle's answer to Dante in canto XIX as to God's inscrutability, namely, if a man has never even heard of Christ, and he is a good man throughout his life and dies without being baptized, why should he be condemned to eternal punishment? Is this divine justice? 'ov'è questa giustizia che 'l condanna? ov'è la colpa sua, se ei non crede?' [Where is this justice that condemns him? Where is his fault if he does not believe?] (*Par.* XIX, 77–8). After having elaborated on God's inscrutable justice in canto XIX, the Eagle mentions in canto XX those souls who were virtuous during their lifetime and were saved. These souls are characterized by the fact that they did not fully comprehend the implications of their good actions, but now that they are in heaven they are fully cognizant.

The first of them, who occupies the Eagle's pupil, is David the psalmist, 'lo cantor dello Spirito Santo' (*Par.* XX, 38), who not only sung the glory of the Lord but also obeyed God without question, such as when he was told to transfer the Arc from Gabaon to Geth and from Geth to Jerusalem. Only now in Paradise he knows the full importance of his actions, 'ora conosce il merto del suo canto' [now he knows the merit of his song] (40). The second is the Emperor Trajan, who consoled a widow by punishing the killers of her son. He spent some time in Hell but now that he is in Paradise he knows the price for not having followed Christ on earth (43–8). The third is Hezekiah, son of David, King of Judea, who was very ill and got his wish to delay his death for fifteen years in order to atone for his sins, 'morte indugiò per vera penitenza' [delayed his death by a true repentance] (51). He knows now that divine judgment is not altered by the prayer of a just man, but that the delay of his death was already foreseen by God, and already part of his destiny (49–54). The fourth soul is the Emperor Constantine, who transferred his rule from Rome to Byzantium in order to make possible the establishment of the Pope's authority in Rome. Constantine now knows that his honest and religious intention, which has always been seen by everyone, including Dante, as the beginning of the corruption and decline of the Church, and the confusion between temporal and spiritual powers, will not be held against him, even though his action brought about endless war and destruction (55–60). The fifth soul is William II the Good, the king of Sicily and Apulia (1169–1189), who is mourned by his people, who, after living under two tyrants, Charles II of Naples and Frederick II of Aragon, also king of Sicily, now knows how just he was (61–6). If all these kings had to learn a different lesson in every case, they are justified in not knowing the extent of their actions since they could not fathom the divine plan that God had for them.

But if in their case we are told why they are in Heaven, in the case of Ripheus the Trojan, we are not. In his case, both he and the reader of the *Commedia* could not fathom the reasons for his presence in the Eagle's pupil. What separates Ripheus from the other major characters mentioned by the Eagle is that he is a minor character in Virgil's *Aeneid*. When he is killed, Virgil writes: 'then Ripheus fell, he who of all the Trojans/ Was most fair-minded, the one who was most regardful of justice' (*Aeneid* II, 426–7). Ripheus's salvation is best explained in terms of *Inferno* I and the warriors Virgil claims died for the well-being of Italy, Camilla, Euryalus, Nisus, and Turnus, but did not, as I have shown in *Reading Dante Reading*. Unlike these warriors, Riphaeus not only did not die as a result of his greed, but he was also a fair and just man, perhaps the only one in the *Aeneid*. But Virgil's attitude towards Ripheus is different from what he showed towards the other warriors. He mourns his death with some regret but does not praise him as he praises the others. 'God's ways are inscrutable' (dis aliter visum), he writes (48). Virgil's words are a sad commentary to the fact that the fair-minded and the righteous have to die. The gods could have saved him but they willed otherwise.

Dante takes up from where Virgil left off, showing, ironically, that if the justice of these false pagan gods ('li dèi falsi e bugiardi') (*Inf.* I, 72) is 'inscrutable' to the extent that it protects the greedy and the violent like Camilla, Euryalus, and Nisus, and not the good and the just like Ripheus, God's justice is 'inscrutable' precisely to the extent that He does exactly the opposite. Ripheus' presence in *Paradiso* is an ironic commentary on Virgil's own poetic justice, which condemns the just and glorifies the unjust.

The cantos of the Heaven of Jupiter conclude with a discourse on predestination and the inability of mortals to guess God's will. Dante uses the examples of Trajan and Ripheus as evidence. In Trajan's case he falls back on the legend that attributed his salvation to the prayers of Gregorius Magnus *(Par.* XX, 106ff). In Ripheus' case, he states that God first revealed to him, as to the Jews, the mystery of future redemption: 'Dio li aperse/l'occhio alla redenzion futura [God opened his eyes to our coming redemption] *(*122–3). Finally, the three theological virtues gave him baptism more than a thousand years before this sacrament was instituted: 'Quelle tre donne li fur per battesmo/ che tu vedesti dalla destra rota, /dinanzi al battezzar piú d'un millesmo' [Those three ladies whom you saw stood by the right wheel for baptism to him more than a thousand years before baptizing] (127–9). The invective, which concludes the canto and the Heaven of Jupiter is directed at those who prejudge arbitrarily who is and who is not to be saved. Even the blessed souls of Paradise who benefit from a direct vision of God do not know who all the elects are: 'ché noi, che Dio vedem,/ non conosciamo ancor tutti li eletti' [for we, who see God, do not yet know all the elect] (134–5).

Yet, the best commentary on the salvation of these two souls comes from the souls themselves, whose lights move along in tune with the words of the Eagle.

> sí, mentre che parlò, sí mi ricorda
>   ch'io vidi le due luci benedette,
>   *pur come batter d'occhi si concorda*
> *con le parole muover le fiammette.*
>   (*Par.* XX, 145–8; emphasis mine)

[so while it spoke, I remember to have seen the two blessed lights, *just as winking eyes keep time together, move with the words their little flames.*]

The analogy of the movement of the two flames that follow the speech of the Eagle winking is not really a comparison. Since the souls of Trajan and Ripheus are part of the Eagle's pupil, their movement is not an analogy but a real occurrence. In other words, as the Eagle speaks they wink, or, which is the same, Dante winks to the reader, to signal that this clever explanation of why the two were saved, especially in Ripheus' case, is not a real explanation. For the reader who understands what Dante is doing here, namely using Ripheus as an example of divine inscrutability, a wink from the poet is meant to get the reader's complicity and acceptance.

The Heaven of Jupiter, which concludes the 'infamous' story of the Eagle as a critique of monarchs and monarchy, is a far cry from what Dante envisaged to be the role and mandate of the monarch in his *Monarchia*. These cantos denounce the utopian ideals of the former treatise, and the fiction of a just ruler whose divine mandate is to be the figurehead of both State and mankind. Here, as elsewhere in Dante's work, the irony is also on the poet and on the illusions he entertained, for himself and others, on the role of Monarchy and of the Monarchs of his time.

7 Heaven of Saturn: Astronomy (XXI–XXII)

E lo cielo di Saturno hae due proprietadi per le quali si può comparare all'Astrologia: l'una si è la tardezza del suo movimento per li dodici segni, ché ventinove anni e più, secondo le scritture de li astrologi, vuole di tempo lo suo cerchio; l'altra si è che sopra tutti li altri pianeti esso è alto. E queste due proprietadi sono ne l'Astrologia: ché nel suo cerchio compiere, cioè ne lo apprendimento di quella, volge grandissimo spazio di tempo; sì per le sue [ancelle], che sono più che d'alcuna de le sopra dette scienze; sì per la esperienza che a ben giudicare in essa si conviene. E ancora: è altissima di tutte le altre, però che, sì come dice Aristotile nel cominciamento de l'Anima, la scienza è alta di nobiltade per la nobiltade del suo subietto e per la sua certezza; e questa più che alcuna de le sopra dette è nobile e alta per nobile e alto subietto, chè de lo movimento del cielo; e alta e nobile per la sua certezza, la quale è sanza ogni difetto, sì come quella che da perfettissimo e regolatissimo principio viene. *E se difetto in lei si crede per alcuno, non è da la sua parte, ma, sì come dice Tolomeo, è per la negligenza nostra, e a quella si dee imputare.* (*Conv.* II, xiii, 28–30; emphasis mine)

[The heaven of Saturn has two properties on account of which it may be compared to Astronomy: the first is the slowness with which it moves through the twelve signs, for, as the astronomers inform us, the time taken by its revolution is more than twenty-nine years; the second is that it is high above all the other planets. Both of these properties are found in Astronomy, too, for a very long period is spent in completing its revolution, that is, in acquiring competence in it, both on account of its ancillary disciplines, which are more numerous than those of the sciences mentioned above, and on account of the experience needed before one can make sound judgments in it. Moreover, this is by far the highest of these sciences, since, as Aristotle says at the beginning of *On the Soul*, a science is exalted in nobility in accordance with the nobility of its subject and the certainty of which it allows; and to a greater extent than any of those mentioned above, this science is noble and high on account of its high and noble subject, the movement of the heavens; it, too, is high and noble on account of the certainty that it allows, which is absolutely free of fault, being generated by an object which is quite perfect in nature and regular in movement. *If anyone thinks he detects a fault in this certainty, this is not to be ascribed to the certainty itself; as Ptolemy remarks, the fault arises rather from our carelessness, and it is to this that it must be imputed.*]

The 7th Heaven of Saturn, which Dante compares to Astronomy, takes only two cantos, XXI and XXII, and they are devoted to the contemplative souls and those with apostolic zeal. The person Dante speaks to is Pietro Damiano, and he is introduced with the usual geographical description of the Benedectine monastery of Fonte Avellana where he was an abbot. Once again the presence of Peter Damiano serves to criticize those monks who no longer live in contemplation for the glory of God, and whose order is now corrupt and in decay:

Render solea quel chiostro a questi cieli
    fertilmente; *e ora è fatto vano,*
    sí che tosto convien che si riveli.
    (*Par.* XXI, 118–20; emphasis mine)

[That cloister used to yield abundant harvest to these heavens, *and now it has become barren so that it must be soon exposed.*]

The last line seems to indicate that something will soon occur to show that the hermitage where Damiano lived has now become sterile, 'vano.' But as Sapegno points out in his commentary the reader is left guessing as to what is really going on. 'Line 120 seems to allude to a precise event, which we do not know anything about, may be the revelation of a scandal, or only a calamity, interpreted by the poet as divine punishment.' However, as we know from previous cases, if Dante announces that something is about to happen it will happen and one should expect it. The problem is that we do not expect Dante to criticize the characters he meets in Paradise, but, as we have seen thus far, this is precisely the case.

From the moment we meet Peter Damiano to the moment we know who he is, as in the case of Cacciaguida, the soul remains hidden, in his joy: 'nascosta/ dentro alla tua letizia' [hidden in your joy] (*Par*. XXI, 55–6). However, as we know by now, whenever the soul is introduced as hidden,' it means that it has something to hide. Furthermore, the use of 'Io veggio ben' [I see well or I understand] (73), always signals Dante's irony since it implies that, on the contrary, he does not understand and that there is more to the issue than meets the eye. Here the irony is in reference to how freely everyone follows divine providence: 'come libero amore in questa corte/basta a seguir la provedenza etterna' [how free love serves in this court for fulfillment of Eternal Providence] (74–5). Even if the allusion is to the souls who in this heaven are free to do as they will, just as Pietro Damiano was free to meet Dante as he came up the ladder of light, Dante still questions it. He wants to know why he was predestined to meet him: 'perché predestinata fosti sola/a questo ufficio tra le tue consorte' [why you alone among your fellows was predestined to this task] (77–8). Instead of an answer, which is delayed because we are in the Heaven of Saturn, we have the introduction of Pietro Damiano and the revelation of which we spoke earlier, 'sí che tosto convien che si riveli' [so that it must be soon exposed] (120). This line is followed by some of the most obscure lines in the poem:

> In quel loco fu 'io Pietro Damiano,
>   e Pietro Peccator fu' nella casa
>   di Nostra Donna in sul lito adriano.
> (*Par*. XXI, 121–3)

[In that place I was Peter Damian, and I was Peter the Sinner in the House of Our Lady on the Adriatic shore.]

The controversy whether Pietro Damiano and Pietro Peccator are two individuals or one and the same has always divided critics, but from the perspective of our general reading of *Paradiso* it is clear that Dante means the two to be the same but different, at least for his own purposes. The reason that Pietro Damiani was introduced as hidden (nascosto) and that this reason would soon be revealed have to do with the reasons why the Monastery of Fonte Avellano is on the decline (fatto vano). Now we can say that the reasons for its decline have to do with Pietro Damiani's leaving the monastery and going 'nella casa' of Nostra Donna 'in sul lito Adriano,' as Pietro Peccator. Dante's reproach is that he left his monastery unattended while he lived elsewhere, signing all his writings, as commentators point out, as 'Petrus peccator.' But besides living in sin, or as a sinner. Pietro's greatest sin was having agreed to become a cardinal late in life, a decision he is made to regret since the position was by then already corrupt.

> Poca vita mortal m'era rimasa,
>   quando fui chiesto e tratto a quel cappello
>   che pur di male in peggio si travasa.
> (*Par.* XXI, 124–6)

[Little of mortal life remained to me when I was sought out and dragged to that hat which is passed on only from bad to worse.]

But, as with the other souls in *Paradiso*, we are dealing here with very minor transgressions. In the case of Peter Damian it is a question of excess of zeal and not because of a desire for earthly glory: 'Non sai tu che tu se' in cielo?/ e non sai tu che 'l cielo è tutto santo,/ e ciò che ci si fa vien da buon zelo? [Don't you know that you are in heaven? Don't you know that heaven is all holy and that whatever is done here comes of righteous zeal?] (*Par.* XXII, 7–9). Peter Damian's sin is 'buon zelo' [righteous zeal], and not gluttony or concupiscence, which, instead, identifies the sins of cardinals and high prelates. Peter's invective against the corruption of these high officials of the Church provides the reason, indirectly, why he went back to Fonte Avellana, but he is still to blame for having chosen, mistakenly, or carelessly, to become a cardinal so late in life.

> Venne Cefàs e venne il gran vasello
>   dello Spirito Santo, magri e scalzi,
>   prendendo il cibo da qualunque ostello.
> Or voglion quinci e quindi chi rincalzi
>   li moderni pastori e chi li meni,
>   tanto son gravi, e chi di retro li alzi.
> Cuopron de' manti loro i palafreni,
>   sí che due bestie van sott'una pelle:
>   oh pazienza che tanto sostieni!'
> (*Par.* XXI, 127–35)

[Cephas came and the great vessel of the Holy Ghost came, lean and barefoot, taking their food at any inn. Now the modern shepherds want one on this side and one on that to prop them up and one to lead them – so portly are they – and one behind to lift their train. They cover their palfreys with their cloaks, so that two beasts go under one skin. O Patience, that have endured so much!']

These high Church officials have degenerated to such a point that they are not different from the animals on which they ride. But their punishment, vengeance (la vendetta) (14), is not far from coming.

> La spada di qua su non taglia in fretta
> né tardo, ma' ch'al parer di colui
> che disiando o temendo l'aspetta.
> (*Par.* XXII, 16–18)

[The sword from here does not strike in haste or tardily, except as it seems to him that awaits it with desire or with fear.]

The vengeance promised by Beatrice, 'la vendetta/ che tu vedrai innanzi che tu muoi' [the vengeance that you will see before you die] (*Par.* XXII, 14–15), is being dealt as she speaks since it comes in the form of Dante's critique as DXV, whose mandate is to expose and punish the degenerate princes of the Church.

Canto XXII features St Benedict, the founder of the Benedictine order, which he founded on Montecassino, as well as the founders of other monastic orders such as Macarius of Alexandria, the chief promoter of Eastern monasticism, and Romualdus of Ravenna, founder of the Order of Camaldoli, or reformed Benedectines. St Benedict is not mentioned by name but only indirectly, through the monastery of Montecassino, which he founded, and through the 'name' of Christ, whose words of love he helped disseminate: 'e quel son io che su vi portai prima/ lo nome di colui che 'n terra addusse/ la verità che tanto ci sublima' [and it was I who first carried up there His name who brought to earth the truth that so exalts us'] (*Par.* XXII, 40–2). The episode also serves as prologue to the final canto of the *Commedia*, because when Dante asks him to reveal himself: 'Però ti priego, e tu, padre, m'accerta/s'io posso prender tanta grazia, ch'io/ti veggia con imagine scoverta' [therefore I pray you, and tell me, father, if I may gain so great a favour, that I may see you with your face unveiled] (58–60), St Benedict tells him that his wish will be fulfilled in the Empyrean. His main function in this Heaven of Saturn is to voice a critique of his order and of other monastic orders in general, their corrupt state, and the decline of the contemplative life, 'e la regola mia/rimasa è per danno delle carte' [my Rule is left to waste the paper] (74–5):

> Le mura che solíeno esser badia
>   fatte sono spelonche, e le cocolle
>   sacca son piene di farina ria.
> (*Par.* XXII, 76–8)

[The walls that were once an abbey have become dens, and the cowls are sacks full of evil flour.]

St Benedict's criticism of his Order is very similar to those of the Franciscans and Benedictines. The abbeys which were once places of contemplation have now become dens of iniquity. What offends most is not so much the decline in spirituality as the greed of the monks who easily forget that all the possessions of the Church (quel frutto) belong to the poor, and they appropriate the funds collected instead of passing them to the needy.

> Ma grave usura tanto non si tolle
>   contra 'l piacer di Dio, quanto quel frutto
>   che fa il cor de' monaci sí folle;
> *ché quantunque la Chiesa guarda, tutto*
>   *è della gente che per Dio dimanda;*
>   *non di parenti né d'altro piú brutto.*
> (*Par.* XXII, 79–84; emphasis mine)

[But heavy usury is not exacted so contrary to God's pleasure as is that fruit which so turns the hearts of the monks to folly; *for all that is in the Church's keeping is for them that ask in God's name, not for kinsfolk or others more vile.*]

Dante is categorical about this last issue, which is the main point of his critique. All that the Church possesses belongs to the poor and to the needy who ask it in the name of Christ, and is not to be lavished on themselves or their kinfolk. The fact that St Benedict's name is not mentioned but is concealed behind the name of Christ is very much to the point. The clergy or the monastic orders are representatives of Christ, and all that belongs to them is to be given away to those who ask it in his name. St Benedict attributes this decadence to the weakness of mortals and exonerates the founders from the sins of their followers and descendants. Human flesh is weak and a strong Order founded by a strong guide such as St Peter or St Francis do not suffice. All these Orders began well but they have slowly deteriorated.

> La carne de' mortali è tanto blanda,
>   che giú non basta buon cominciamento
>   dal nascer della quercia al far la ghianda.
> Pier cominciò sanz'oro e sanz'argento,
>   e io con orazione e con digiuno,
>   e Francesco umilmente il suo convento.
> E se guardi il principio di ciascuno,
>   poscia riguardi là dov'è trascorso,
>   tu vederai del bianco fatto bruno.
>   (*Par.* XXII, 85–93)

[So soft is mortal flesh that a good beginning below does not last from the springing of the oak to the bearing of the acorn. Peter began his fellowship without gold or silver, and I mine with prayer and fasting, and Francis his with humility; and if thou look at the starting point of each, then look again whither it has strayed, you shall see it from white becoming brown.]

Only a miracle can revert this process. This is the hope on which St Benedict's invective ends. There have been many miracles in the past, and perhaps another will reverse this trend.

> *Veramente* Iordan volto retrorso
>   piú fu, e 'l mar fuggir, quando Dio volse,
>   mirabile a veder *che qui 'l soccorso.*
>   (*Par.* XXII, 94–6; emphasis mine)

[*Truly*, Jordan was driven back and the sea turned back when God willed it, these were sights more wondrous than succor here.]

The conceit here is that the withdrawal of the waters of Jordan to let the Israelites led by Joshua advance, or the opening of the Red Sea to let Moses through, are great wonders, just as a return to the old Rules would be for monastic orders, if God willed it. But this apparent hope conceals a final irony because the miracle would not be to reverse the downward flow of monastic orders, but to change human nature!

'Truly' (Veramente), God can stop rivers from flowing and seas to open, but he cannot change human nature and cannot make mortal flesh strong which is by nature weak. Even God cannot make this miracle: 'che qui 'l soccorso'!

Canto XXII concludes with an apostrophe to the reader and one last look at the earth, which from the height of Saturn appears so insignificant that Dante cannot help but smile, 'tal, ch'io sorrisi del suo vil sembiante' [such that I smiled at its vile appearance'] (*Par.* XXII, 135), at the thought that men would kill each other to gain a piece of it: 'L'aiuola che ci fa tanto feroci' [the little threshing floor that makes us so fierce'] (151).

The Heaven of Saturn extends Dante's critique of the Church, and, more specifically, of the monastic orders to include the last major order of St Benedict and the Benedictines, and it paves the way for Dante's 'examination' of the theological virtues, faith, hope, and charity, in the Heaven of Fixed Stars.

8 Fixed Stars: Physics and Metaphysics (XXIV–XXVII)

Dico che lo Cielo stellato si puote comparare a la Fisica per tre proprietadi, e a la Metafisica per altre tre: ch'ello ci mostra di sé due visibili cose, sì come le molte stelle, e sì come la Galassia, cioè quello bianco cerchio che lo vulgo chiama la Via di Sa' Iacopo; e mostraci l'uno de li poli, e l'altro tiene ascoso; e mostraci uno suo movimento, da oriente ad occidente, e un altro, che fa da occidente ad oriente, quasi ci tiene ascoso. Per che per ordine è da vedere prima la comparazione de la Fisica, e poi quella de la Metafisica. [...] Ancora: per lo polo che vedemo significa le cose sensibili, de le quali, universalmente pigliandole, tratta la Fisica; e per lo polo che non vedemo significa le cose che sono sanza materia, che non sono sensibili, de le quali tratta la Metafisica; e però ha lo detto Cielo similitudine con l'una scienza e con l'altra. Ancora: per li due movimenti significa queste due scienze. Ché, per lo movimento ne lo quale ogni die si rivolve e fa nova circolazione di punto a punto, significa le cose naturali corruttibili, che cotidianamente compiono loro via, e la loro materia si muta di forma in forma; e di queste tratta la Fisica. E per lo movimento quasi insensibile che fa da occidente in oriente per uno grado in cento anni, significa le cose incorruttibili, le quali ebbero da Dio cominciamento di creazione e non averanno fine; e di queste tratta la Metafiisica. Però dico che questo movimento significa quelle, che essa circulazione cominciò e non avrebbe fine, ché fine de la circulazione è redire ad uno medesimo punto, al quale non tornerà questo cielo, secondo questo movimento. E così è manifesto che lo Cielo stellato, per molte proprietadi, si può comparare a la Fisica e a la Metafisica. (*Conv.* II, xiv, 1–2, 9–13)

[I declare that the Heaven of Fixed Stars may be compared to Physics on account of three properties, and to Metaphysics on account of another three.

For it displays to us two features visible within it, the multitudinous stars and the Galaxy, that is, the white circle popularly known as St James' Way; and it displays to us one of its movements, that from east to west, while keeping almost hidden from us its other movement, from west to east. And so I must explain the similarities first with Physics, then with Metaphysics [...] Furthermore, the pole of this heaven which we see signifies things that can be perceived by the senses, which form the subject of Physics; and the pole which we do not see signifies things which are without matter, things which cannot be perceived by the senses, which form the subject of Metaphysics. For this reason, then, the heaven under discussion has a close similarity to each of these sciences. Moreover, by its movements it signifies these two sciences. For by the movement in which it every day goes through a revolution, and circles anew to the very point from which it started, it signifies those things of nature which are subject to decay, which day by day complete their passage and have their matter transferred from one form to another; these are what Physics considers. By the almost imperceptible movement this heaven makes from west to east, shifting one degree in a hundred years, it signifies beings not subject to decay, which had a beginning through God's act of creation but will never have an end; these are what Metaphysics considers. Consequently, I declare that this movement signifies these beings in that their revolution comes to an end when it returns to the same point, a point which this heaven in pursuing this movement will never reach. For since the beginning of the world little more than a sixth of the revolution has been completed, while we live in the final stage of history, and indeed in expectation of the consummation of the movement of the heavens. It is clear, then, that the Heaven of Fixed Stars may on account of many properties be compared to Physics and Metaphysics.]

As with the Cacciaguida cantos, in the Heaven of Fixed Stars we are dealing with another set of three cantos. These are the cantos where Dante is examined on his knowledge of the three theological virtues: faith, hope and charity, respectively, by St Peter (*Par.* XXIV), St James (*Par.* XXV), and St John (*Par.* XXVI).

Appropriately this set of cantos begins by reiterating the main function of the *Paradiso*, and of the *Commedia*, providing the reader with vital nourishment.

> 'O sodalizio eletto alla gran cena
>   del benedetto Agnello, il qual vi ciba
>   sí, che la vostra voglia è sempre piena,

> se per grazia di Dio questi preliba
>   di quel che cade della vostra mensa,
>   prima che morte tempo li prescriba,
>   ponete mente all'affezione immensa,
> e roratelo alquanto: *voi bevete*
>   *sempre del fonte onde vien quel ch'ei pensa.'*
> (*Par.* XXIV, 1–9; emphasis mine)

[O fellowship elect to the great supper of the blessed Lamb, who feeds you so that your desire is ever satisfied, since by God's grace this man has foretaste of that which falls from your table, before death appoints his time, give heed to his measureless craving, and bedew him some drops; *you drink ever of the fountain whence comes that which he thinks.*]

Beatrice's words emphasize the didactic role of Dante's poetic allegory that the poet elaborates from the first chapter of the *Convivio*, where he describes the purpose and function of his poetic banquet. The 'vivande' that the reader will savour are his often misunderstood allegorical *canzoni*, which the poet will explain with the bread of his commentary. The nourishment, in the cantos of the Heaven of Fixed Stars, relates to Dante being examined on the three theological virtues by St Peter, St James, and St John, who personify these virtues.

The modality of the nourishment is determined by the movements of this heaven, which corresponds to the sciences of Physics and Metaphysics, whose movements are, respectively, visible and invisible: 'e mostraci l'uno de li poli, e l'altro tiene ascoso; e mostraci uno suo movimento, da oriente ad occidente, e un altro, che fa da occidente ad oriente, quasi ci tiene ascoso' [and it displays to us one of its movements, that from east to west, while keeping almost hidden from us its other movement, from west to east]. Physics is the science of things that can be perceived by the senses, and signifies those things which are subject to decay. Metaphysics, instead, considers those things that are not perceptible to the senses and are not subject to decay.

The blessed souls Dante meets in this heaven partake of this duality of heaven and earth, as one of their aspects is visible and can be perceived by the senses, and the other is not. St Peter, for example, is both the holder of the keys of the blessed council in heaven: 'Quivi triunfa [...] colui che tien le chiavi di tal gloria' [Here [...] he triumphs in his victory who hold the keys of such glory] (*Par.* XXIII, 136–9) and the holder of the keys of God's council on earth, as he is the founder of the Church. Besides the 'heavenly' St Peter who examines Dante on faith, the reader can expect a 'human' side of St Peter which is not visible and immediately perceivable by the senses.

The discrepancy between these two sides generates the irony of these cantos, especially when it is Peter who examines Dante on the virtue of faith, when, as is generally well-known, he is the one among all apostles who actually lacked it. As we read in Matthew XIV: 28–9, in the famous episode of walking on water, when Jesus invited him to walk off the boat onto the water, Peter went, at first, but as he saw that the wind was strong, he became afraid, and because he was sinking, he cried: 'Lord, help me!' And Jesus helped him, saying: 'You man of little faith, why have you doubted me?' When Beatrice encourages Dante to ask St Peter what is faith, she alludes, precisely, to this episode:

tenta costui di punti lievi e gravi,
  come ti piace, intorno della fede,
  per la qual tu su per lo mare andavi.
  (*Par.* XXIV, 37–9; emphasis mine)

[test this man on points light and grave as you see good regarding the faith *by which you walked the sea.*]

The irony is not limited to this episode but characterizes Peter's entire examination on faith. One form taken by this irony is in asserting the authority of Paul over Peter as the commander-in-chief, the 'alto primopilo' [the High Commander] (*Par.* XXIV, 59), and as the real authority (*'l verace stilo*) in matters of faith. In other words, if this had been a real examination, St Paul should have asked the questions, whereas in this canto he only provides the answers, through Dante. The situation is, in fact, reversed. Rather than the examiner, Peter becomes the student to whom Dante teaches, through St Paul, what is faith. The possibility of this reversal, as I have indicated, is inherent to the Heaven of Fixed Stars where we are dealing with two movements, one visible and the other hidden. Thus, instead of viewing St Peter's questions as a test for Dante, we should read these questions as a way of instructing him on what is faith. In fact, the term 'to examine' is never used. Dante uses 'tenta,' which can mean 'try' or 'tempt,' which is just what Jesus did to test Peter's faith by asking him to walk on water, unsuccessfully.

> *tenta* costui di punti lievi e gravi,
>   come ti piace, intorno della fede,
>   *per la qual tu su per lo mare andavi.*
>   (*Par.* XXIV, 37–9; emphasis mine)

[test this man on points light and grave, as pleases you, concerning the Faith by which you did walk upon the sea.]

These lines reiterate, ironically, Peter's failure to pass his examination on faith when Jesus tested him. Now, in Paradise, he is being tested again.

Dante's answer to Peter's first question, What is faith? – 'Di' buon cristiano, fatti manifesto:/ fede che è?' [Speak, good Christian, declare yourself. What is faith?] (*Par.* XXIV, 52–3) – is from Paul to the Hebrews 11:1.

> E seguitai: 'Come *'l verace stilo*
>   ne scrisse, padre, del tuo caro frate
>   che mise teco Roma nel buon filo,
> fede è sustanza di cose sperate
>   ed argomento delle non parventi;
>   e questa pare a me sua quidditate.'
>   (*Par.* XXIV, 61–6; emphasis mine)

[And I went on: 'As the *truthful pen* of your dear brother wrote, who with you, father, put Rome on the good path, Faith is the substance of things hoped for and the evidence of things not seen; and this I take to be its essence.']

St Paul is described here as the one who possesses true authority, ' 'l verace stilo,' and the brother that with Peter set Rome on the rightful course of the proper faith. As commentators have remarked, Dante is alluding to a sentence in Peter's Second Letter, 'So also our beloved brother Paul wrote to you according to the wisdom given him, speaking of this as he does in all his letters' [sicut et carissimus frater noster Paulus, secundum datam sibi sapientiam, scripsit vobis] (2 Peter 3:14). Here, of course, there is no mention of setting Rome on its proper course. In fact, the point of Dante's irony is that Peter never set Rome and Christianity on its proper course, whereas Paul did, especially when we consider that he is Rome's first pope, the 'gran viro/ a cui Nostro Signor lasciò le chiavi' [the great man with whom our Lord left the keys] (*Par.* XXIV, 34–5). Peter's second letter, usually thought to be written by one of his disciples, is usually known as the letter against false prophets where it is said that 'false prophets also arose among the people, just as there will be false teachers among you, who will secretly bring in destructive heresies, even denying the Master who bought them, bringing upon themselves swift destruction' (2 Peter 2:1). Whether Dante, in referring to Peter's Second Letter, meant to allude to Peter as a false prophet or a false teacher, we will never know, but we do know that as a teacher of faith Peter is a false teacher, and that he also denied his Master, Christ.

Peter's second question to Dante is a clarification of Paul's previous definition of faith, namely, why Paul placed Faith first among substances and later among arguments:

Allora udi': 'Dirittamente senti,
   se bene intendi perchè la ripose
   tra le sustanze, e poi tra li argomenti.'
(*Par.* XXIV, 67–9)

[Then I heard: 'You think rightly if you understand well why he placed it among substances and after among evidences.']

The answer is that on earth the mysteries of the faith are hidden, and so faith functions as the substance or the foundation of what is hoped. We call faith 'argomento' because from this faith we can argue the reality of these mysteries, with a similar certainty that we employ in syllogisms.

E io appresso: 'Le profonde cose
   che mi largiscon qui la lor parvenza,
   alli occhi di là giú son sí ascose,
che l'esser loro v'è in sola credenza,
   sopra la qual si fonda l'alta spene;
   e però di sustanza prende intenza.
E da questa credenza ci convene
   sillogizzar, sanz'avere altra vista;

però intenza d'argomento tene.'
(*Par.* XXIV, 70–8)

[And I then: 'The deep things which so richly manifest themselves to me here are so hidden from men's eyes below that there their existence lies in belief alone, on which is based the lofty hope; and therefore it takes the character of substance. And from this belief we must reason, without seeing more; therefore it holds the character of evidence.']

Peter's reply only goes to contribute to the humour of this canto to a level equaled only by the encounter between Virgil and Statius in *Purgatory* XXI and XXII (see my *Reading Dante Reading*). Peter replies that if people understood the workings of faith the way Dante has just outlined them there would be no place for sophisms: 'Se quantunque s'acquista/ giù per dottrina, fosse così inteso,/ non li avría loco ingegno di sofista' [If whatever passes for doctrine down below would be so understood there would be no room for sophistry] (*Par.* XXIV, 79–81). What Peter is stating, or is made to state, is precisely his own case, as he never believed or had faith in the mysteries that Jesus revealed to the apostles.

In pure comic fashion, and in ways which remind us once again of the ironic encounter between Virgil and Statius, Peter wants to know on what foundation Dante's faith rests: 'Questa cara gioia/ sopra la quale ogni virtú si fonda,/ onde ti venne?' [This precious jewel on which every virtue rests, whence did it come to you?] (*Par.* XXIV, 89–91). Dante's answer is that faith is founded on the word of the Holy Ghost, which permeates the pages of the Old and New Testaments. This evidence is sufficient proof that any claim to the contrary is false, 'ogne dimostrazion mi pare ottusa' [every demonstration seems obtuse to me] (96). But Peter is relentless. He wants to know why Dante believes that these texts are inspired by the word of God, 'perché l'hai tu per divina favella?' [why do you hold them for the divine word] (99). For Dante the proof rests on the miracles that confirm them, 'La prova che 'l ver mi dischiude/ son l'opere seguite' [The proof which declares the truth to me is the works that followed] (100–1). Peter, once again, in a manner typical of the man of little faith, asks for proof that those miracles really occurred: 'chi t'assicura/ che quell'opere fosser?' [who assures you that these works ever were?] (*Par.* XXII, 103–4). Dante mentions, as the greatest miracle and sufficient proof, the number of people that converted to Christianity. The real miracle, however, is that

Christianity was spread by simple people like Peter who planted the seed which became a vine, which is now sterile: 'ché tu intrasti povero e digiuno in campo, a seminar la buona pianta/che fu già vite e ora è fatta pruno' [for you entered the field poor and fasting to sow the good plant that was once a vine and is now become a thorn] (*Par.* XXIV, 109–11). Once again, Dante's irony is aimed at Peter, and all the popes who followed him, with the implication that nothing good has ever come from the institution that Peter founded. Instead of cultivating the vine of God, his successors have destroyed it.

Finally, Peter asks for evidence for the object of his faith, the single things he believes in and how he obtained them: 'ma or convene spremer quel che credi,/ e onde alla credenza tua s'offerse' [but now you must declare what you believe and from where you obtained this belief] (*Par.* XXIV, 122–3). The episode recalls Virgil's words to Statius concerning how he became a Christian, and the latter replying that his conversion occurred while reading Virgil's works. Dante answers the last question by alluding first to the famous episode when Peter and John rushed to the Sepulcher where Jesus was buried, but He was not to be found.

> 'O santo padre, spirito che vedi
> ciò che credesti sí che tu vincesti
> ver lo sepulcro piú giovani piedi.'
> (*Par.* XXIV, 124–6)

[O holy father, spirit who sees what you believed so that you did outstrip younger feet to the sepulcher.]

As those commentators point out, who believe that Dante got it wrong, the opposite is the case. When Mary Magdalene tells Peter and John that Jesus has vanished, they both head off for the Sepulcher, but it is John who arrives first. However, since neither of them understands what has happened, that Jesus has resurrected from the dead, they return home (John XX: 3–9). The episode is another example of Peter's lack of faith, since he does not hurry to the Sepulcher but lets his younger brother get ahead of him. The episode is ironical, not only because it states that Peter won (vincesti) the race to the Sepulcher, when he did not, but also because he states that he believes what he sees. One may be tempted to believe that Peter believed he could see, but since we know that he did not believe, for which reason he did not hurry to the

Sepulcher, he did not see anything, or, which is the same, since he did not believe he did not see anything. But the main irony is that the example is supposed to serve as the basis for Dante's own faith, 'onde alla credenza tua s'offerse' [whence it was offered to your belief] (*Par.* XXIV, 123).

Peter's examination of Dante on Faith denounces indirectly Peter's own lack of faith, and becomes Dante's way to instruct, by means of Paul, not only the reader but Peter himself, on the subject of faith. In this examination, Peter becomes the pupil, but the lesson is also directed to the popes that succeeded him, who, like Peter, also lacked faith.

In fact, the figure of St Peter is reintroduced in canto XXVII in a final invective against the popes, and, in particular, Boniface VIII.

> Quelli ch' usurpa in terra *il luogo mio,*
>   *il luogo mio, il luogo mio,* che vaca
> nella presenza del Figliuol di Dio,
> fatt'ha del cimiterio mio cloaca
>   del sangue e della puzza; onde 'l perverso
>   che cadde di qua su, là giù si placa.'
> (*Par.* XXVII, 22–7; emphasis mine)

[He who on earth usurps *my place, my place, my place,* which in the sight of the Son of God is vacant, has made my burial ground a sewer of blood and stench, so that the Perverse One who fell from here above takes comfort there below.]

Yet, once again, the indirect target of the passage is Peter, who is at the origin of the corruption of the Church. Even though what is being stated is meant to apply to Boniface VIII, it is to Peter as the founder of the Church and to his burial place, which has now become a sewer of blood and stench, that the passage, ironically, refers to and condemns. In an ironic reversal, Peter's famous three times denial of Christ is echoed here in the three time repetition of 'luogo mio,' which is both his burial ground and the place where the Church was founded. The repetition not only condemns Peter but also underscores the fact that the Church is in fact founded on the denial of Christ. That is why Peter's place is empty of the presence of Christ: 'che vaca/ nella presenza del Figliuol di Dio.' Rather than housing Christ, Peter's place is inhabited by Lucifer, the rebel angel, ' 'l perverso,' who after falling from grace found more suitable surroundings in the Church,

Peter's 'place,' 'là giú si placa.' That is why, ashamed of his three time denial of Christ, and of the generation of popes he has produced, Peter's face changes colour:

> quand'io udi': '*Se io mi trascoloro,*
>   non ti maravigliar; che dicend'io
>   vedrai trascolorar tutti costoro.
> (*Par.* XXVII, 19–21; emphasis mine)

[when I heard, '*If I change colour*, marvel not, for, as I speak, you shall see all of them change colour.]

St Peter's invective against his successor Boniface VIII is Dante's ironic way to finally undermine Peter as the origin of all the evil that has plagued the Church since its inception. Peter's denial of Christ not only characterizes his successors, who similarly deny Christ with their office, but is also the reason why Christ is absent from the Church, and why the Church has become a den of perversion and evil, where Satan thrives. Peter's invective against the generation of popes that followed him (40–66) outlines by negation all the iniquities committed by the popes and how they strayed from the mandate that Christ had given to Peter and to them. The first part of the invective underlines the greed that corrupted the martyrdom of his first successors:

> '*Non fu la sposa di Cristo allevata*
>   del sangue mio, di Lin, di quel di Cleto,
>   *per essere ad acquisto d'oro usata.*
> (*Par.* XXVII, 40–2; emphasis mine)

[*The spouse of Christ was not nurtured* on my blood and that of Linus and Cletus, *to be employed for gain of gold.*]

The second part of the invective is aimed at the division created by the Church in taking sides and dividing the populace in Guelphs and Ghibellines, and in promoting civil war.

> *Non fu nostra intenzion* ch'a destra mano
>   de' nostri successor parte sedesse,
>   parte dall'altra del popol cristiano;
> (*Par.* XXVII, 46–8; emphasis mine)

[*It was not our purpose* that one part of the Christian people should sit on the right of our successors, and one part on the left;]

In the third part, Peter's invective addresses the plague of the civil wars and the role played by the Church, which ought to be fighting infidels and not other Christians:

né che le chiavi che mi fuor concesse
   divenisser signaculo in vessillo
   che *contra battezzati combattesse.*
   (*Par.* XXVII, 49–51; emphasis mine)

[nor that the keys which were committed to me should become the ensign on a banner for *warfare on the baptized.*]

The fourth part condemns the practice of simony, and, in particular, the use of his image in the papal seal to sell privileges.

né che io fossi figura di sigillo
   a privilegi venduti e mendaci,
   ond'io sovente arrosso e disfavillo.
   (*Par.* XXVII, 52–4; emphasis mine)

[*Nor that I should be made a figure on a seal* to be sold and lying privileges, whereat *I often blush and flush.*]

Of course, this last invective is the final irony at Peter's expense. The reason he is embarrassed is not so much because popes engage in simony but because his image is used on the papal seal. Peter would rather not be known as the founding father of these 'rapacious wolves in shepherd's garb' (*Par.* XXVII, 55).

It is against these 'lupi rapaci' that St Peter's invective finally concludes, not only to condemn the present state of the Church but also to look forward to its imminent divine punishment:

In vesta di pastor lupi rapaci
   si veggion di qua su per tutti i paschi.
   o difesa di Dio, perché pur giaci?
   (*Par.* XXVII, 55–7; emphasis mine)

[Rapacious wolves in shepherd's garb can be seen from here in every pasture. O *defense of God, why do you lie still?*]

The invocation to God to intervene to punish the shepherds of His flock brings us back to the punitive role and function of the DXV, which is to expose and to condemn the injustices and the corruption in the Church and in the Empire. St Peter's final words and his instruction to Dante to make his knowledge known addresses and fulfils the task of the DXV.

> Ma l'alta provedenza che con Scipio
>   difese a Roma la gloria del mondo,
>   *soccorrà tosto, sì com'io concipio.*
> e tu figliuol, che per lo mortal pondo
>   ancor giú tornerai, *apri la bocca,*
>   *e non nasconder quel ch'io non ascondo.'*
> (*Par.* XXVII, 61–6; emphasis mine)

[But the high Providence, which with Scipio defended for Rome the glory of the world, *will succor swiftly, as I conceive it*. And you, my son, who, because of your mortal weight, will again return below, *open your mouth and do not hide what I hide not.*']

These lines reiterate the punitive action of the DXV, and the Veltro, whose justice is as immediate ('tosto') as the revelation of the deceit of even the most pious and holy men, as here with St Peter.

* * *

In canto XXV Dante is examined on the theological virtue of Hope by St James. The canto opens with the poet's hope that his poem 'al quale ha posto mano e cielo e terra' [to which both heaven and earth have set their hand] (*Par.* XXV, 2), will win over his enemies who have exiled him, 'la crudeltà che fuor mi serra' [the cruelty that bars me from the fair sheepfold] (4), so that he may return to Florence to receive his poetic laurel in his beloved Church of San Giovanni. However, since we know that Dante, at the time he wrote this canto, knew that he had no hope of ever returning to Florence, this statement of hope, in a canto on hope, serves the opposite purpose, and undermines, from the start, any possibility of hope.

As in the previous canto on Faith, where Peter is hardly a figure of Faith, in this canto, similarly, James' role as a figure of Hope is equally questionable. Beatrice's emphasis on this very fact makes his role even more suspicious: 'Inclita vita [...] fa risonar la spene in questa altezza;/ tu sai, che tante fiate *la figuri,*/quante Iesú ai tre fe' piú carezza' [Illustrious living soul [...] make hope resound in his height; you know, who many times were the *figure* when Jesus of the three showed most favour to you] (*Par.* XXV, 29–33). Whenever in the *Commedia* a statement is accompanied with 'tu sai' [you know], it is almost certain that the opposite is the case, and that, on the contrary, it means that it is not so. What we do know is that James is one of the three apostles, with Peter and John, who always accompanied Jesus in his wanderings: at the Transfiguration (Matthew 17: 1–8), in the Garden of Gethsemane (26: 36–8), and at the rising of the daughter of Jairus (Luke 8: 50–6). But there is really no evidence that James is the figure of Hope, except for the fact that Busnelli, a modern editor of the *Commedia*, assures us that the three apostles represent the virtues of Faith, Hope, and Charity. (See Busnelli's commentary to *Par.* XXV, 29–33.)

The only reference to a text by James, which is really not by him, but we are told was considered his in the Middle Ages, is the *Epistle of James*, to which Dante alludes in answering James' question: What is hope and where did it originate?: 'di' quel ch'ell'è, e come se ne 'nfiora/ la mente tua, e dì onde a te venne' [tell me what it is and how it blossoms in your mind, and tell me from where you got it] (*Par.* XXV, 46–7):

> Tu mi stillasti, con lo stillar suo,
>   ne la pistola poi.
>   (*Par.* XXV, 76–7)

[You, in your epistle, instilled it in me, after his instilling.]

Dante's answer is that what gave him hope, after reading David's Psalm IX:11 (lo stillar suo) quoted verbatim by Dante, '"Sperino in te," nella sua teodia/dice "color che sanno il nome tuo"' [Let them hope in Thee who know Thy name, he says in his divine song] (73–4), was James' letter. However, as every commentator points out, the epistle does not deal with the theme of Hope but with enduring one's trials with steadfastness. James' question reminds us of Virgil's question to Statius in *Purgatory* XXIII of how he became a Christian. Statius' surprise answer, that he converted by reading Virgil's *Eclogue*, finds an echo in Dante's claim that he found hope in James' epistle, which is equally without foundation. The indirect message, however, is that while Dante had lost all hope, he is enduring his exile with steadfastness.

As *Paradiso* XXIV serves to denounce Peter's lack of Faith, rather than to demonstrate Dante's Faith, something very much the same is at work in this canto. Of the three questions that James asks Dante on Hope: 'What is hope, to what extent he possesses it, and from where he derives it?' only the second one is answered by Beatrice, who suddenly intervenes before the pilgrim can even speak. Commentators believe this is because it would have been too conceited of Dante if he had replied himself, when in fact, as Beatrice relates, no one, among Militant Christians, is more hopeful than Dante, and for this reason he is allowed to undertake this journey, before his time.

> 'La Chiesa militante alcun figliuolo
>   non ha con più speranza, *com'è scritto*
>   nel sol che raggia tutto nostro stuolo:
> però li è conceduto che d'Egitto
>   vegna in Ierusalemme, per vedere,
>   anzi che 'l militar li sia prescritto.
>   (*Par.* XXV, 52–7; emphasis mine)

[The Church Militant has not a child more full of hope, *as is written* in the Sun that irradiates all our host; therefore it is granted to him to come from Egypt to Jerusalem that he may see it before his service is accomplished.]

It would certainly be quite a boast on Dante's part, if this were, indeed, the correct reading. Beatrice's statement, however, has to be seen first of all within the parameters of the irony of the canto and in terms of the initial disavowal by Dante of any hope of ever returning to Florence. The statement should also be viewed in terms of the last cantos of *Purgatory* and the DXV, which, as I have shown, points to the poet's mandate to denounce the corrupt state of the Church and the Empire. Within this context, Beatrice's words allude to the fulfillment of Dante's hope, which is actualized 'as is written' (com'è scritto) in his critique of souls like Cacciaguida and, now, the Apostles. In fact, the first reference to Psalm 121, echoed in the words of James: 'Leva la testa e fa che t'assicuri' [Lift your head and let me assure you] (34) is not very reassuring, since the Psalm does not contain a message of hope but of despair: 'I lift up my eyes to the hills. From whence does my help come?' In the Psalm, of course, the help to David comes from the Lord. In canto XXV help and hope should come, supposedly, from James. In Dante's case, however, hope comes to him only from Virgil, as indicated in the following lines, which echo a similar passage in *Inferno* II: 'Questo conforto del foco secondo/mi venne; ond'io levai li occhi a' monti/che li 'ncurvaron pria col troppo pondo' [This assurance came to me from the second fire; therefore I lifted up my eyes to the hills whose greatness weighed them down before] (*Par.* XXV, 37–9). These lines, which describe Dante lifting his eyes comforted by James's words, recall a similar episode in *Inferno* II when Virgil comforts the poet with the story of the three ladies who consent to his journey through the three realms: 'Tu m'hai con disiderio il cor disposto/ sì al venir con le parole tue,/ch'i' son tornato nel primo proposto' (*Inf.* II, 135–8). However, as I have indicated in my analysis of this passage, Dante's renewed hope does not come from divine will, but is very much grounded in his own poetic powers represented by Beatrice and the 'donna gentile,' which are only figures for poetry and philosophy, respectively. Dante's hope is not in any divine intervention but in the strength of his own poetic powers, which dictate that he take the roundabout way around the mountain, through the realms of Hell, Purgatory, and Paradise. It is in this sense that Dante's initial 'hope' at the beginning of *Paradiso* XXV to return to Florence becomes a reality: 'con altra voce omai, con altro vello/ ritornerò poeta' [with another voice and with another fleece, I will return poet] (*Par.* XXV, 7–8). He will return to Florence, not physically and not as when he left it, but metaphorically, with another poetic voice, that of allegory, and another 'vello,' that of the *Commedia*.

What is hopeless, on the contrary, is precisely what at the beginning of the poem, in *Inferno* I, was the ambition and arrogance of his wish to go up the mountain alone, an error associated with the biased poetics of Virgil's *Aeneid*. A similar delusion and hopelessness awaits those that put their hope in James, since the hills that Dante sees are really Peter and James: 'ond'io levai li occhi a' monti/ che li 'ncurvaron pria col troppo pondo' [whereon I lifted up my eyes unto the hills which had curved them before with excess weight] (*Par.* XXV, 38–9). In the end, the definition of Hope that Dante provides is straight out of Peter Lombard, and is a 'certain' expectation of his own future poetic glory: ' "Spene" diss'io 'è uno attender certo/ della gloria futura' [Hope, I said, is a sure expectation of future glory (67–8)].

James' fourth question to Dante is: 'What does Hope promise you': 'ed èmmi a grato che tu diche/quello che la speranza ti 'mpromette'

[I would be grateful if you told me what hope has promised you] (*Par.* XXV, 86–7). Dante's answer, according to some commentator, relates to what the Old and New Testaments point out to be blessedness in Heaven, namely, perfect joy of the body and the spirit. Dante in fact quotes Isaiah 61:7 to the effect that every soul in their land possesses a 'double garment' (doppia vesta), and their land (la sua terra) is this heavenly paradise.

> Dice Isaia che ciascuna vestita
> *nella sua terra fia di doppia vesta;*
> e la sua terra è questa dolce vita.
> (*Par.* XXV, 91–3; emphasis mine)

[Isaiah says that each *in his own land shall be clothed with a double garment,* and their land is this sweet life.]

Line 92, however, is controversial because the verse from Isaiah speaks of a 'double portion': 'Instead of your shame you shall have a double portion,' Commentators, in general, believe in fact that Dante gets it wrong, and that he mistranslates the passage. However, experience with reading Dante teaches us that most often, if not every time, whenever we think Dante is misreading or mistranslating a text, it is because we have not fully understood his poetic intention. This may well be one of these cases. First of all, the lines double the phrase 'sua terra,' which is repeated twice in lines 92 and 93. While we can read 'sua terra' as just meaning 'heaven,' it is clear that the repetition wants also to indicate the two lands, earth and heaven, where in one the dress is the body, in the other it is the soul. This 'double' focus is a characteristic of this Heaven of Fixed Stars, as I have indicated, where one movement is visible and belongs to the earth, and to Physics; the other is invisible and belongs to heaven, and to Metaphysics; and where one is in decay, the other is eternal. The same principle is at work in canto XXV with the double movement of the figure of James and St James. Yet, in this case, as later with John and St John, we are dealing with souls whose bodies cannot be found. It is as if we had St James, but not James, St John but not John.

In the case of James, we know that after spending some time in Spain, in Campostello, he returned to Jerusalem where he was martyred by Herod Agrippa. Dante writes of St James as early as the *Vita Nova*, XL (7), where he recalls the pilgrims that journey to visit the tomb of

St James in Santiago de Campostella: 'non s'intende peregrino se non chi va verso la casa di sa' Iacopo o riede' [pilgrims are those who go or come from the house of St James]. Dante distinguishes the pilgrims, who go to St James' tomb, from the 'palmieri,' who just go abroad, and 'i romei,' who go to Rome, and he adds that St James' burial place is far from his country of origin: 'però che la sepultura di sa' Iacopo fue più lontana de la sua patria che d'alcuno altro apostolo' [though St James' burial is further away from his country than any other apostle]. Legend has it that while St James was martyred in Jerusalem, his body was miraculously transferred to Santiago de Campostella, then the capital of Galicia. The relics, Singleton reports, were discovered by Theodomir, bishop of Iria, who was guided to the spot by a star, hence the name Campus Stellae, field of the stars. Dante quotes as evidence what John, James' brother, wrote in Revelation 7:13 about the souls of the elect gathered at the last judgment wearing 'white robes.'

> E 'l tuo fratello assai vie più digesta,
>   là dove tratta delle *bianche stole*,
>   questa revelazion ci manifesta.'
>   (*Par.* XXV, 94–6; emphasis mine)

> [And your brother, where he tells of the *white robes*, declares this revelation to us far more expressly.]

After the Resurrection, writes Singleton, the body will become 'bright and pure like the spirit, and will share in its happiness.' The white robes are the bright bodies of the blessed souls who will appear together with the other souls at the Final Judgment. As a result, a legend became very popular that St John had not died but had gone to heaven with his body. But as Dante is being questioned by James, St John appears, suddenly, to disavow all that has been said about him, and in answer to Dante, who is trying to figure out whether St John is in Heaven with his body or not, he sets the record straight.

> *In terra terra è 'l mio corpo, e saràgli*
>   *tanto con li altri, che 'l numero nostro*
>   *con l'etterno proposito s'agguagli.*
>   Con le due stole nel beato chiostro
>   son le due luci sole che saliro;
>   *e questo apporterai nel mondo vostro."*
>   (*Par.* XXV, 124–9; emphasis mine)

[*My body is earth on earth,* and it will be there with the rest till our number tallies with the eternal purpose. With the two robes in the blessed cloister are only the two lights that have ascended, and this *report you shall take back to your world.*]

John declares false the legend that would have him in Heaven in body and soul, and retracts his own prophecy. Only Christ and the Virgin Mary are in Heaven in body and soul. As for the apostles, they will have to wait for Judgment Day, not until, that is, the number of the blessed will equal the number pre-established in the mind of God.

The sudden irruption of St John on the scene puts an end to Dante's hopes and to James' examination, since what Hope promises, we now know, is without foundation. John's intervention also solves the question of where James' body lies. Dante simply confirms his belief stated in the *Vita Nova* that James' body is not in Campostello but is separated from its place of origin, which, in the *Commedia* and in *Paradiso* XXV, means precisely what John is made to admit, namely, that body and soul are separated at death, and that one is on earth and the other is in heaven. What appeared to be a mistranslation on Dante's part of *Isaiah* 61, of 'double robes' instead of 'double portion,' turns out to be a correct reading. As the lines indicate with the repetition of 'sua terra,' which is usually read literally as 'questa dolce vita,' meaning Heaven, two places are meant, one on earth for the body and the other on Heaven for the soul; thus, 'two robes.' In other words, the promise of hope, which rests on John's 'bianche stole' [white robes] (*Par.* XXV, 95), is essentially unfounded. Through St John's intervention and admission, Dante undermines the entire concept of Hope and James' representation of it.

* * *

Though St John makes his appearance in canto XXV, it is in canto XXVI that he examines Dante on the virtue of Charity. The entire interview occurs, however, when Dante is in a state of blindness, having lost his vision by staring at St John's flame, hoping to see his body. This is the metaphysical level of this canto, but the physical level has to do with Saul's blindness after being struck on the road to Damascus, and with his conversion from Saul to Paul by Ananias touching his eyes and restoring him to sight. In my analysis of *Inferno* II (32), 'Io non Enea, io non Paulo sono' [I am not Aeneas, I am not Paul], I have already indicated how the reference to Saul's conversion parallels the story of

Dante, who convinced by Virgil's words of the 'three women' (tre donne), decides to undertake the journey. In *Paradiso* XXVI (12), Beatrice's instrumental role in convincing Dante to undertake the journey, or to write the poem, is recognized as the virtue possessed by Ananias' hands, 'la virtù ch'ebbe la man d'Anania' [the same virtue that had the hand of Ananias] (*Par.* XXVI, 12) Beatrice's virtue, as Dante's Ananias, is 'love,' but as Dante's answer to St John's questions reveals, this is not the love that he celebrated in the *Vita Nuova*, but a love which presupposes a 'love' of philosophy, of the 'donna gentile,' mentioned by Virgil in his account in *Inferno* II. As Ananias, Beatrice is the mediatrix, the physical aspect of the metaphysical force behind it, which in Paul's case is God and in Dante's case is philosophy, or love of wisdom.

In this canto on charity, Dante celebrates his love for philosophy through the poetic figure of Beatrice as Ananias, who dispelled the blindness that characterized his early works and restored his 'sight' to enable him to write a poem, the *Commedia*, which celebrates his love of wisdom, under the aegis of allegorical poetry: 'quand'ella entrò col foco ond'io sempr'ardo' [when she entered with the fire with which I always burn] (*Par.* XXVI, 15).

In answer to St John's question concerning what is charity, or what is the object of Dante's love: 'e di' ove s' appunta/l'anima tua' [and say on what aim your soul is set] (*Par.* XXVI, 7–8), Dante alludes to the Paolo and Francesca episode of *Inferno* V, 'scrittura/mi legge Amore' [the writing that Love reads to me] (17–18). This time, however, the reference is to the Love (of philosophy) that inspires him and dictates to him, and not to the Love as tyrant, as in the case of Paolo and Francesca. This is Dante's new Love, the beginning and the end of all his writings: 'Alfa ed O è di quanta scrittura' [the alpha and omega is of how much writing] (17).

St John's second question encourages Dante to be more clear as to who is responsible for his new poetic undertaking: 'dicer convienti/ chi drizzò l'arco tuo a tal berzaglio." [you must tell me who directed your bow to that target'] (*Par.* XXVI, 22–4). His answer, indirectly, and once again, is philosophy, love of wisdom:

> E io: 'Per filosofici argomenti
>   e per autorità che quinci scende
>   cotale amor convien che in me s'imprenti
> (*Par.* XXVI, 25–7)

[And I: 'By philosophic arguments and by the authority that descends from here, such love must needs imprint itself on me]

St John's question: 'Ma di' ancor se tu senti altre corde/ tirarti verso di lui' [but tell me further if you feel other cords pull you to him] (*Par.* XXVI, 49–50) brings us back to the beginning of the poem and to Dante's state of blindness, which almost caused his 'death,' and from which the love of philosophy saved him.

> con la predetta conoscenza viva,
>   tratto m'hanno del mar dell'amor torto,
>   e del diritto m'han posto alla riva
>   (*Par.* XXVI, 61–3)

[with the living assurance of which I spoke, they have drawn me from the sea of perverse love and have brought me to the shore of the love that is just]

The lines recall Dante's near drowning in the 'pelago' in the first canto of the poem, which alludes to Dante's error in the *Vita nuova,* for having engaged in a false conception of love as pleasure (amor torto), typical of Guido Guinizelli and the so-called school of the 'dolce stil nuovo.' With the help of his new love, and through the mediation of Beatrice as Ananias, the 'scales' of Dante's blindness fall off and he sees again with a new light:

> così de li occhi miei ogne quisquilia
>   fugò Beatrice col raggio d'i suoi,
>   che rifulgea da più di mille milia
> *onde mei che dinanzi vidi poi;*
>   (*Par.* XXVI, 76–9; emphasis mine)

(thus Beatrice chased away every mote from my eyes with the radiance of her own, which shone more than a thousand miles; *so that I then saw better than before;*)

Dante's new 'sight' is the new allegorical understanding which he acquires through philosophy and which allows him to forge a new poetics and a new understanding of the nature of wisdom, love, and virtue.

* * *

Canto XXVI concludes with the introduction of the figure of Adam. In this brief parenthesis, Adam poses the questions, which Dante has supposedly formulated in his own mind, and answers them. Dante's encounter with Adam, as expected, is not without irony. His first lines to him: E cominciai: 'O pomo che maturo/solo prodotto fosti' [O fruit that were alone produced mature] (*Par.* XXVI, 91–2) point to Adam's guilt of having shared the apple with Eve, and, consequently, his lack of maturity. But Dante makes Adam confess an even more important flaw:

> Or, figliuol mio, non il gustar del legno
> fu per sé la cagion di tanto essilio,
> ma *solamente il trapassar del segno*.
> (*Par.* XXVI, 115–17; emphasis mine)

> [Now know, my son, that the tasting of the tree was not in itself the cause of so long an exile, but only *the passing of the sign*.]

The lines recall the flaw of Ulysses, who foolishly went beyond the pillars of Hercules that set the limits of the world; but, as I have indicated in my analysis of *Inferno* XXVI, which parallels this canto, the verses do not imply self-sacrifice in the name of knowledge. Ulysses is not condemned to Hell for having striven for knowledge, but he is punished for having deceived his companions, who followed him to their death persuaded by his false promises of knowledge and virtue. Similarly, Adam's flaw is to have led men to (know) death through his act of pride (as death was the punishment for having disobeyed God's law) disguised as an act of knowledge.

The most important aspect of Adam's speech, however, is reserved for language, and here, of course, the indirect reference is to *De vulgari eloquentia* and its similarity and difference from this canto. One major difference is the admission that Adam's language was extinct before Nimrod attempted to build the Tower of Babel, while in the Latin treatise, Dante had claimed that Adam's language was still spoken until the confusion of languages, and after that by the Jews alone. The reason for this shift is given in the next few lines: 'ché nullo effetto mai razionabile,/ per lo piacere uman che rinovella/seguendo il cielo, sempre fu durabile' [for never was any product of reason durable forever, because of human pleasure that changes constantly following the heavens] (*Par.* XXVI, 127–9). Because of human nature, which is variable, no product of man can ever remain permanent for long. Language is no exception. While it is natural for man to speak, how man speaks depends on man alone:

Opera naturale è ch'uom favella;
   ma cosí o cosí, natura lascia
   poi fare a voi secondo che v'abbella.
Pria ch'i' scendessi all'infernale ambascia,
   I s'appellava in terra il sommo bene
   onde vien la letizia che mi fascia;
e *El* si chiamò poi; e ciò convene,
   ché l'uso de' mortali è come fronda
   in ramo, che sen va e altra vene.
(*Par.* XXVI, 130–8)

[That man should speak is nature's doing, but whether thus or thus, nature then leaves you to follow your own pleasure. Before I descended to the anguish of Hell the Supreme Good from whom comes the joy that swathes me was named *I* on earth; and later He was called *El*: and that must needs be, for the usage of mortals is as a leaf on a branch, which grows away and another comes.]

Though language is natural, its usage is arbitrary because man attributes different meanings to different sounds, as he sees fit, and this usage changes from men to men, from people to people, and from epoch to epoch. As a corrective to *De vulgari eloquentiae*, Dante proposes, through Adam, a theory of language as sign, which, as I have indicated already, points to his new theory of poetry as allegory.

In these cantos of the Heaven of Fixed Stars nothing is really fixed. The figures that embody 'fixed' examples of faith, hope, and charity, turn out to be just the opposite. Rather than showing that St Peter, St James and St John possess knowledge of these virtues, Dante denounces their shortcomings precisely in these virtues, and far from being the one who is being examined, he teaches the wisdom of how to read ironically.

9 Primum Mobile: Moral Philosophy (XXVII–XXIX)

Lo Cielo cristallino, che per Primo Mobile dinanzi è contato, ha comparazione assai manifesta a la Morale Filosofia; ché Morale Filosofia, secondo che dice Tommaso sopra lo secondo de l'Etica, ordina noi a l'altre scienze. Ché, sì come dice lo Filosofo nel quinto de l'Etica, 'la giustizia legale ordina le scienze ad apprendere, e comanda, perché non siano abbandonate, quelle essere apprese e ammaestrate'; e cosí lo detto Cielo ordina col suo movimento la cotidiana revoluzione di tutti li altri, per la quale ogni die tutti quelli ricevono [e mandano] qua giù la vertude di tutte le loro parti; ché, se la rivoluzione di questo non ordinasse ciò, poco di loro virtude qua giù verrebbe o di loro vista. Onde ponemo che possibile fosse questo nono Cielo non muoere, la terza parte del Cielo [stellato] sarebbe ancora non veduta in ciascun luogo de la terra; e Saturno sarebbe quattordici anni e mezzo a ciascuno luogo de la terra celato, e Giove sei anni quasi si celerebbe, e Marte uno anno quasi, e lo Sole centottantadue dì e quattordici ore (dico'dì, cioè tanto tempo quanto misurano cotanto dì) e Venere e Mercurio quasi come lo Sole si celerebbe e mosterebbe, e la Luna per tempo di quattordici dì e mezzo starebbe ascosa ad ogni gente. E da vero non sarebbe qua giù, né vita d'animale o di piante; notte non sarebbe né die, né settimana né mese né anno, ma tutto l'universo sarebbe disordinato, e lo movimento de li altri sarebbe indarno. E non altrimenti, cessando la Morale Filosofia, l'altre scienze sarebbero celate alcuno tempo, e non sarebbe generazione né vita di felicitade, e indarno sarebbero scritte e per antico trovate. Per che assai è manifesto questo cielo sé avere a la Morale Filosofia comparazione. (*Conv.* II, xiv, 14–19)

[The Crystalline Heaven, described as the First Moving Body in the account given above, is quite clearly similar to Moral Philosophy, because, as Thomas says in his commentary on the second book of *Ethics*, Moral

Philosophy directs us towards the other sciences. For, as the Philosopher states in the fifth book of the *Ethics*, 'civic justice directs that the sciences be learned in due order, and, to ensure that they never be abandoned, commands that they be both learned and taught'; similarly the heaven just mentioned directs with its movements the daily revolution of all the others, by which means all those heavens every day receive and communicate to our world below the power invested in their every part, for if the revolution of this heaven did not direct this, little of their power would come down to our world below, and we would have little sight of them. Consequently, in the hypothetical case that this ninth heaven did not move, a third of the Heaven of the Stars would not yet have been seen from any place on earth; Saturn would be hidden from every place on earth for fourteen and a half years; Jupiter would be hidden for almost six years, Mars for almost a year, the Sun for one hundred and eighty-two days and fourteen hours. Venus and Mercury would be hidden and be visible for much the same time as the Sun, and the Moon would remain concealed from all mankind for fourteen and a half days. And, indeed, in this world below, plant and animal life would neither be generated nor continue; there would be neither night nor day, nor weeks, months, or years, and in fact the whole universe would be thrown into disorder, and the movement of other heavens would be in vain. In the same way, should Moral Philosophy disappear, the other sciences would be hidden for some time, the life of happiness would neither be generated nor continue, and it would have been in vain that the sciences were discovered in ancient times and committed to writing. It is quite clear, then, that this heaven has a similarity to Moral Philosophy.]

The Primum Mobile, or Crystalline Heaven, is the heaven which imparts motion to the other heavens and from which everything else in the universe originates:

'La natura del mondo, che quieta
  il mezzo e tutto l'altro intorno move,
  quindi comincia come da sua meta.
  (*Par.* XXVII, 106–8)

[The nature of the universe, which holds the centre quiet and moves all the rest around it, begins here as from its starting point.]

The Primum Mobile contains no bodies, stars, or planets; it is the outermost of the moving spheres, and has no other place but the mind of

God. Its motion comes from Divine Love, which transmits virtue to all other spheres:

> e questo cielo non ha altro dove
> che la mente divina, in che s'accende
> l'amor che il volge e la vertú ch'ei piove.
> *(Par.* XXVII, 109–11)

[And this heaven has no other where than divine mind, where is kindled the love that revolves it.]

The Primum Mobile is responsible for directing the daily revolution of all the planets, and should this not occur, little of their power would come down to earth, and we would have only a partial sight of them. These characteristics make this heaven comparable to Moral Philosophy, which similarly directs us towards the other sciences and imparts its virtue to them. In the event that Moral Philosophy should disappear, the sciences themselves would disappear and there would be chaos and unhappiness: 'the life of happiness would neither be generated nor continue, and it would have been in vain that sciences were discovered in ancient times and committed to writing' (*Conv.* II, xiv, 18).

The perfect and diaphanous working of the Primum Mobile, however, is far from being similar to the relationship between Moral Philosophy and the other sciences. Instead of comparing the workings of this heaven to the way the will of God and virtue are transmitted to all the spheres, and, in particular to mankind, Dante describes the workings of 'greed' (cupidigia), which underlies all human actions, rather than the love of God.

> Oh cupidigia che i mortali affonde
> sí sotto te, che nessuno ha podere
> di trarre li occhi fuor de le tue onde!
> Ben fiorisce nelli uomini il volere;
> ma la pioggia continua converte
> in bozzacchioni le susine vere.
> *(Par.* XXVII, 121–6)

[O greed, who so plunge mortals in your depths that none has power to lift his eyes from your waves! The will blossoms in men, but the continual rain turns the good plumbs into blighted fruit.]

Man's will is directed towards the good, but being weak it is easily swayed and corrupted by greed. Greed, and its symbol the 'lupa' [she-wolf], is man's fundamental flaw, which is not only at home in *Inferno*, where we expect it, and in *Purgatory*, but also in *Paradiso*, as we have seen. Faith and innocence are only to be found among the very young, who lose both as soon as they are barely grown up.

> Fede ed innocenzia son reperte
>   solo ne' parvoletti; poi ciascuna
>   pria fugge che le guance sian coperte.
> (*Par.* XXVII, 127–9)

[Faith and innocence are found only in small children; then each flies away before the cheeks are covered.]

As soon as man has barely grown a beard, he begins a life of excess, he becomes a glutton, has no longer any respect for his mother, and wishes her dead.

> Tale, *balbuziendo ancor*, digiuna,
>   che poi divora, con *la lingua sciolta*,
>   qualunque cibo per qualunque luna;
> e tal, *balbuziendo*, ama e ascolta
>   la madre sua, che, *con loquela intera*,
>   disai poi di vederla sepolta.
> (*Par.* XXVII, 130–5; emphasis mine)

[One, *as long as he stammers* he fasts, afterward, when his *tongue is free, he* devours any food through any month. And one, *while he stammers*, he loves his mother and listens to her, afterward, when *his speech is whole*, he longs to see her dead.]

This bleak view of man's nature turned greedy and violent, as soon as he is barely free of his mother's care, is not the whole story. It constitutes only the first term of a comparison (Tale ... e tal), which has its second term in the last tercet of the canto which begins appropriately with 'Così':

> Così si fa la pelle bianca nera
>   nel primo aspetto della bella figlia

di quel ch'apporta mane lascia sera.
(*Par.* XXVII, 136–8)

[So the white skin turns black at the first sight of the fair daughter of him that brings morning and leaves evening.]

These verses, as Sapegno acknowledges in his commentary, are 'one of the most arcane Dantesque enigmas' (uno dei più chiusi enigmi danteschi). The difficulty stems, in part, from the fact that they are usually read in isolation and separate from the comparison of which they are part. But the key to understanding these verses is the emphasis which is placed on language, which is said to go from stammering to full and free flowing speech. This process recalls, unmistakably, the 'femmina balba' of *Purgatory* XIX, which, as I indicated in my analysis of the episode in *Reading Dante Reading* (see chap. 4, 77ff), points to the deceit inherent in language that turns man into a siren, and makes him the dupe of his own language. The point that Dante wants to make is that desire begins in and with language. As long as man stammers he has faith and he is innocent. The moment he acquires the ability to speak he is led astray by his own language, and he is seduced, unknowingly, in desiring what is most harmful to him and to others. So he becomes a glutton, devouring everything around him, or greedy, desiring whatever is most harmful to him or wishing his mother dead. This incomprehensible act against someone who gave him life and should be most dear to him becomes understandable when we realize that one's mother is, perhaps, the only person who can restrain him and lead him back to reason and virtue. A mother is potentially the one major obstacle to man's fulfillment of his most abject desires.

To understand the full implications of the comparison, and of the last tercet, it is important to keep in mind the allusion to Ulysses, to which the 'femmina balba' episode alludes, and to whom Dante refers, indirectly, in this canto, as that 'varco folle di Ulisse' [the mad passage of Ulysses] (*Par.* XXVII, 82–3). Ulysses recalls the other siren, Circe, the witch that kept him from his homeland, and was also the beautiful daughter (bella figlia) of the Sun (quel che apporta mane e lascia sera).

Dante wants to say that man, once he has acquired full control of his speech, becomes his own siren (like Ulysses) and turns himself into an animal, or into a pig (like Circe turned Ulysses' companions into pigs), devouring everything in sight ('divora ... qualunque cibo per qualunque luna'). In this condition, man is comparable to Circe, who changed her outer aspect ('primo aspetto') from that of a kind woman into a siren, that is, from white to black (fa la pelle bianca nera), and turned Ulysses' companions into pigs. Singleton, who comes very close to solving the enigma does not, however, take into account the destructive power of language. Here are his conclusions:

> Beatrice is saying that the white skin of human nature (the innocent child) turns 'black' (i.e., is corrupted by sinful desire) as soon as it looks upon worldly goods, that is, at the first sight of them ('primo aspetto'), in their power to tempt. (See Singleton's commentary to lines 136–8.)

The point of the comparison, which is not really a comparison but only a pseudo-simile, as Singleton would say, is to situate the origins of man's greed in language, in rhetorical language. As long as man stammers he is safe from himself, but when he begins to exercise his power of speech, when he becomes an adept at using language, he becomes easily deceived by his own rhetoric, which persuades him that what is harmful to him is what is best for him. He becomes the dupe of his own language, which deceives him into believing in the reality of the fiction that he has himself created. He becomes his own siren and his own Circe, and by doing away with reason and rational thought, he descends to the level of animal.

The truth of what Dante states is as inevitable as it is incontrovertible. This process cannot be reversed, as in the Ulysses-Circe episode, or interrupted, as in Dante's case in *Purgatory* XIX. Man's self-deception is something that one can be aware of but cannot resolve. In *Purgatory* XIX even Virgil is incapable of preventing Dante from being seduced by his own language. Only Lucy can save him:

> Ancor non era sua bocca richiusa,
>   quand'una donna apparve santa e presta
>   lunghesso me per far colei *confusa*.
> (*Purg.* XIX, 25–7; emphasis mine)

> [Her mouth was not yet shut when a lady, holy and alert, appeared close beside me to *confound* her.]

Lucy saves him by confounding the language that was holding Dante hostage. However, this is impossible, both for Ulysses, who becomes the victim of his own rhetoric ('il varco folle d'Ulisse'), as well as for his companions, whom he has so well persuaded that it would have been impossible even for him to persuade them to turn back: 'Li miei compagni fec'io sì arguti,/con questa orazion picciola, al cammino,/ che a pena poscia li avrei ritenuti' [I made my companions so keen for the journey, with my brief talk, that barely I could have held them back] (*Inf.* XXVI, 121–3). It is similarly impossible for man. The language of self-mystification is so compelling that nothing confounds it, short of one's death, or of those who stand in its way, including one's mother.

Dante suggests one possibility that may revert this process, and this is a solution for which he had opted in the *Monarchia*, where he had claimed that the monarch, whom he compared to the Primum Mobile, can rule both the Empire and mankind.

> And since the whole sphere of heaven is guided by a single movement (i.e., that of the Primum Mobile), and by a single source of motion (who is God), in all its own parts [...] mankind is in its ideal state when it is guided by a single ruler (as by a single source of motion) and in accordance with a single law (as by a single movement) in its own causes of movement and in its own movements. (*Monarchia* I, ix, ii-iii)

In *Paradiso* XXVII, one of the reasons for the widespread corruption is said to be the lack of a monarch, who, as the Primum Mobile, would guide and unite under his virtuous guidance both Empire and the family of man, 'pensa che 'n terra non è chi governi;/ onde sí svia l'umana famiglia [consider that on earth there is no one who governs, wherefore the human family goes thus astray (*Par.* XXVII, 140–1). The last line of the canto suggests just this possibility, that a new leader at the helm of the ship of State might reverse the course of human nature.

> che *la fortuna* che tanto s'aspetta,
>   le poppe volgerà u' son le prore,
>   sì che la classe correrà diretta;
> *e vero frutto verrà dopo 'l fiore.'*
>   (*Par.* XXVII, 146–8; emphasis mine)

> [that the *storm* which we have been waiting shall turn round the sterns to where the prows are, so that the fleet shall run straight; *and true fruit will come after the flower.*]

The term 'fortuna' is ambiguous here. In English it has always been translated as 'storm' because only a storm, an act of Nature or of God, can turn the ship, and man's nature, around. The storm as an act of nature, like 'fortuna,' can either redirect the ship to safety or can destroy it. Similarly, a just ruler may redirect man on his 'diritta via' to its ultimate goal, which is God, or he may not, as is often the case, as we have seen. The last line,'e vero frutto verrà dopo 'l fiore,' appears to lean towards a positive outcome. Just as the true fruit comes after the flower, so will safety after a storm. Similarly, the intervention of a monarch, assisted by God, could be instrumental in reversing the destructive course of human nature. The improbability of such an occurrence, however, is made clear from the flower/fruit imagery, which states the possibility of a true fruit in reverse, 'e vero frutto verrà dopo 'l fiore.' In the verse, the fruit comes first and then the flower, denoting not only a process that goes against nature, but also the impossibility of the process altogether. Yet, there may be hope. The emphasis is on 'vero frutto' (true fruit), which does not point just to any fruit but only to the 'true' one. Only a 'true' flower, that is, a virtuous nature, may blossom and give fruit, not just everyone. The example recalls the beginning of *Paradiso*, where Dante tells his readers that only a few people can follow his journey, the others can do so at their own peril.

> O voi che siete in piccioletta barca,
>   desiderosi d'ascoltar, seguiti
>   dietro al mio legno che *cantando varca*,
> tornate a riveder li vostri liti;
>   non vi mettete in pelago, ché *forse*,
>   perdendo me, rimmareste smarriti.
>   (*Par.* II, 1–6; emphasis mine)

> [O you that are in your little bark, full of desire to hear, following behind my ship that *singing makes its way*, turn back to see again your shores ... Do not commit yourselves to the open sea, that *may be*, if you lost me you would go astray.]

As I indicated in Prologue II, these lines are an allusion to the beginning of *Convivio* and to the poet's warning that not everyone is invited to his banquet, because not everyone will be able to understand his commentary to the *canzoni*. Similarly, not everyone can follow the poet in his journey because not everyone will be able to understand his allegorical message. The danger is alluded to in that 'cantando varca,' which recalls, once again, 'il varco d'Ulisse' (*Par.* XXVII, 82–3) and Ulysses' companions who perished under similar circumstances. A similar fate may attend those who let themselves be seduced by the siren-like sweet song of his poetry and get lost, 'may be' (forse). Just as Dante in the *Convivio* invited to his banquet only a select few, in the *Paradiso* he invites only those few who, as Boethius in his *Consolation of Philosophy*, have been able to resist the seductive advances of poetry and to love the wisdom of Lady philosophy.

> *Voialtri pochi che drizzaste il collo*
>   *per tempo al pan de li angeli,* del quale
>   vivesi qui ma non sen vien satollo,
> metter potete ben per l'altro sale
>   vostro navigio
>   (*Par.* II, 10–14)

[*You few who lifted up your necks in time to the bread of angels*, on which one feeds but are never sated, you may indeed commit your vessel to the deep sea.]

Only those who have learned from Dante's teachings to read his poetry allegorically, for the poetic wisdom it contains, can hazard to read him. Only these flowers will bear a 'true fruit,' perhaps.

To believe, or to desire that human nature can change, is to believe in the fiction of our own language, and to disregard the example of Ulysses and his companions, and the tragic fate that awaits those who are seduced by a promise of knowledge. When we really consider 'our origins,' as Ulysses exhorted his companions to do, we realize that our human nature cannot change by acquiring knowledge, as he promised, and that knowledge does not bring virtue. This is man's illusion, and his self-deceit. The examples of Dante himself in the *Convivio*, Brunetto Latini or Ulysses are good illustrations of the error to which man easily falls prey. This is the substance of Dante's teachings, of the wisdom that his *Commedia* imparts to the reader who is not seduced by the mesmerizing sweet song of his poetry. This is a wisdom that alerts us to the mystifications inherent in the promise of knowledge, and to the self-deceit inherent in our desire to achieve it. It is not by chance that the metaphor for the 'bread of angels,' which gives us nourishment and of which we will never have enough – 'del quale vivesi qui ma non sen vien satollo' – is the same as the metaphor for greed, as symbolized by the she-wolf: 'Ed una lupa, che di tutte brame/ sembiava carca ne la sua magrezza' [And a she-wolf, that in her leanness seemed full with every craving'] (*Inf.* I, 49–50). Both the thirst for knowledge, of which we never grow satisfied, and greed which makes us always desire for more, are but two sides of the same process. The wisdom that Dante's *Commedia* teaches depends on the extent to which we understand this difference.

Canto XXVII marks a radical departure from the claims Dante made in *Monarchia*, of a ruler who will unite under his rule both Empire and the family of man. In the treatise, human nature appears to be of secondary importance and not a hindrance to the rule of the monarch, as Primum Mobile of the Empire and mankind:

> Again, every son is in a good (indeed ideal) state when he follows in the footsteps of a perfect father, *insofar as his own nature allows (in quantum propria natura permictit)*. Mankind is the son of heaven, which is quite perfect in all its workings; for man and the sun generate man, as we read in the second book of the *Physics*. Therefore mankind is in its ideal state when it follows the footsteps of heaven, *insofar as its nature allows (in quantum propria natura permictit)*. (*Monarchia* I, ix, i-ii; emphasis mine)

In the *Monarchia*, the role of mankind is minor and insignificant, and seems as if it can be easily dismissed. But what appears to be an innocent qualification in *Monarchia*, which can be easily ignored, as it has always been, in the *Commedia*, and especially in this Heaven of Heavens, it assumes paramount importance and not only affects the workings of mankind but the very balance of power between monarchs and popes, Church and Empire. Greed, which is the basic trait of human nature, becomes the great stumbling block to the monarch's fulfillment of his divine mandate. This means that the Primum Mobile, as well as the *Paradiso*, not only functions as a corrective to *Monarchia*, but it is evidence that the political treatise must well antedate the cantica, if not the *Commedia*.

* * *

Paradiso XXVIII begins under the aegis of specularity by reintroducing the myth of Narcissus of *Paradiso* III, where Dante had claimed to have committed his contrary error. Whereas Narcissus took his reflection to be real, Dante, believing that what he saw was a reflection of the blessed souls, turned around but saw nothing. In *Paradiso* XXVIII, when Dante turns around he finds that the reflection and the object correspond perfectly, 'e vede ch'el s'accorda/con esso come nota con suo metro' [and sees that it accords with it as a song with its measure] (*Par.* XXVIII, 8–9). However, while the created world is modelled on the heavenly world, they are anything but similar. Why this is so, now Dante wants to know, 'udir convienmi ancor come l'essemplo/ e l'essemplare come non vanno d'un modo' [I would like to hear further why the model and the copy do not go in one fashion] (55–6). A comparison, replies Beatrice, must not be based on appearances, which are different, but on their virtue, 'se tu alla virtú circonde/la tua misura, *non alla parvenza*' [if you draw your measure round the virtue, *not to the semblance*] (73–4; emphasis mine). But confusion still plagues Dante, especially as to the order of the celestial hierarchy. He appears to side with Dionysius in *De Caelesti Hierarchia*, even though in the *Convivio* he had sided with Gregory. In this canto, Gregory admits that he was wrong once he saw for himself, and laughed at his own mistake, 'sí tosto come li occhi aperse/in questo ciel, di sé medesmo rise' [as soon as he opened his eyes in this heaven, he smiled at himself (134–5)]. The canto ends by establishing a textual correspondence between the truth (ver), which Dionysius was able to discern on earth, and the truth (ver), which can be attested in this heaven.

> E se tanto secreto *ver* proferse
>   mortale in terra, non voglio ch'ammiri;
>   ché chi 'l vide qua sù gliel discoperse
> con altro assai del *ver* di questi giri.
>   (*Par.* XXVIII, 136–9; emphasis mine)

> [And if a mortal declared on earth so much secret *truth*, I would not have you wonder, for he who saw it here on high disclosed it to him, with much more *truth* about these circles.]

The correspondence between the 'ver' on earth and the 'ver' in heaven is meant to establish the validity of Dionysius' truth claim, which now finds confirmation in heaven. This should come as no surprise, states Beatrice, because the hierarchical ordering of the angels was revealed to Dionysius by St Paul, who learned of it when he was 'caught up to the third heaven' (Corinthians II, 12:2–4).

However, if there is perfect correspondence between what is claimed by Dionysius of the hierarchical ordering of angels and what we find in heaven, there are discrepancies between human and angelic faculties and Canto XXIX is devoted essentially to a critique of angelology and of those who presume to know the nature of angels.

> Ma perché in terra per le vostre scole
> *si legge che l'angelica natura*
> *è tal, che 'ntende e si ricorda e vole,*
> ancor dirò, *perché tu veggi pura*
> *la verità che là giú si confonde,*
> *equivocando in sí fatta lettura.*
> (*Par.* XXIX 70–5; emphasis mine)

[But since it is taught in your schools on earth that *the angelic nature is such that it understands and remembers and wills*, I will speak further, *in order that you may see in purity the truth that down there is confounded by the equivocation in such teachings.*]

Dante's main argument is that angelic seeing (vedere), in its gaze of God, was never interfered with to the point that its vision was divided (diviso) and memory was necessary. Of course, the exception are the rebel angels that Dante deals with in passing. The number of these intelligences from the creation to their rebellion is insignificant, he states ironically, as they hardly amount to twenty: 'Né giugneriesi, numerando, al venti' [Counting, you would not reach twenty] (*Par.* XXIX, 49). Even though their impact has been devastating, as their rebellion disrupted the entire fabric of man's nature: 'turbò il suggetto d'i vostri alimenti' [disturbed the basis of your elements] (51). Dante's irony is clear, but the subject of human nature has been so amply discussed throughout the *Commedia* that Dante does not need to further elaborate on it here.

The remaining angels maintained a perfect correspondence with God so that their vision is direct and not interfered with by any object, 'non hanno veder interciso/ da novo obietto' [do not have their vision interfered by a new object] (*Par.* XXIX, 79–80), so they do not need to remember as a result of a difference between image and concept, 'e però non bisogna/ rememorar per concetto diviso' [so they do not need remembering as a result of a divided concept] (80–1). The contrary is the case on earth, where men live in a perpetual dream and under the illusion that they have discovered the truth:

> sí che là giú, non dormendo, si sogna,
>   credendo e non credendo dicer vero.
> (*Par.* XXIX, 82–3)

> [so that down there men dream while awake, believing and not believing to be speaking the truth.]

Dante has in mind those philosophers who, whether they believe or not in what they are saying, led by a desire to appear ingenious and original, do not follow the path of truth, which is only one: 'Voi non andate giù per un sentero/ filosofando' [You do not proceed along one path in philosophizing] (85–6). Philosophers get carried away by appearances and by thoughts of glory and ambition, 'tanto vi trasporta/ l'amor dell'apparenza e 'l suo pensiero!' [So much does the love of appearances and its thought carries you away!] (86–7). If this is a veiled critique of Dante's beloved philosopher, Aristotle (lo Filosofo), we shall never know, but it is possible. After all, Aristotle's claim, quoted at the beginning of the *Convivio* that 'man naturally desires to know […] because science is the ultimate perfection of our soul, in which our happiness resides' (*Conv.* I, i), is a lot similar to what is claimed by Ulysses when trying to persuade his companions, with the well-known tragic consequences.

A worse distortion, however, is when men either dismiss or willfully distort the true word of God, which is written in the Old and the New Testaments, 'quando è posposta/la divina scrittura, o quando è torta' [when divine scripture is set aside or even perverted (*Par.* XXIX, 89–90)]. The culprits are the preachers who distort the truth to their advantage:

> Per apparer ciascun s'ingegna e face
>   sue invenzioni; e quelle son trascorse
>   da' predicanti e 'l Vangelo si tace.
> (*Par.* XXIX, 94–6)

> [Everyone strives for appearances and makes his inventions, and these are picked up by the preachers and the Gospel is silent.]

These preachers like to spread fairy tales (favole) instead of the word of God, with the result that the flock ('pecorelle) returns from pasture full of empty air (pasciute di vento) instead of being nourished by the word of God. Ignorance here is no excuse. Christ did not say to his apostles to go and preach nonsense (ciance) (110), but He gave them a true foundation, 'ma diede lor verace fondamento' (111). Preaching has now become an end in itself, and all for the glory and the ambition of those who preach.

> Ora si va con motti e con iscede
> a predicare, e pur che ben si rida,
> gonfia il cappuccio, e piú non si richiede.
> (*Par.* XXIX, 115–17)

[Now men go forth to preach with jests and buffooneries, and as long as one laughs, and fills up the cowl, nothing more is asked.]

People accept unquestioningly the indulgences sold by these preachers without asking if what they promise can be delivered. Dante has in mind the monks of St Anthony, who grow fat on the charity and offerings they receive in exchange for their worthless indulgences.

> Di questo ingrassa il porco sant'Antonio,
> e altri assai che sono ancor piú porci,
> pagando di moneta sanza conio.
> (*Par.* XXIX, 124–6)

[On this St Anthony's pig fattens, and others also, who are even more pigs, paying with money that has no coinage.]

Dante's final exhortation to the reader is to keep aiming at the right way (la dritta via) (128), even if one happens to be very far from it, in the hope that with time the distance will shorten: 'sí che la via col tempo si raccorci'(129). This view reiterates what was said in the previous canto of the 'vero fiore,': those 'few' who with luck and perseverance may turn their boat around and deliver a 'fruit.'

In this Crystalline Heaven, or Primum Mobile, based on an analogy with Moral philosophy, not everything is crystal clear. Greed, ambition, and love of glory are the motivating forces that move the world of men rather than divine love or love of God. The problem seems to be a lack of guidance both at the religious level and at the political level. There is no emperor or pope that can lead men both politically and spiritually. Dante's critique, as DXV, of both Church and Empire proves not only the impossibility of a future remedy to this situation, but also identifies the source of this malaise in greed, which affects man as soon as he is old enough to speak. It is in times such as these, when mankind is without guidance, that poetry finds its true prophetic voice in the ironic language of poetic allegory.

10 Empyrean: Theology (XXX–XXXIII)

Ancora: lo Cielo empireo per la sua pace simiglia la Divina Scienza, che piena è di tutta pace; la quale non soffera lite alcuna d'oppinioni o di sofistici argomenti, per la eccellentissima certezza del suo subietto, lo quale è Dio. E di questa dice Esso a li suoi discepoli: 'La pace mia do a voi, la pace mia lascio a voi,' dando e lasciando a loro la sua dottrina, che è questa scienza di cu' io parlo. Di costei dice Salomone: 'Sessanta sono le regine, e ottanta l'amiche concubine; e de le ancille adolescenti non è numero: una è la colomba mia e la perfetta mia.' Tutte scienze chiama regine e drude e ancille; e questa chiama colomba perché è sanza macula di lite, e questa chiama perfetta perché perfettamente ne fa il vero vedere nel quale si cheta l'anima nostra. (*Conv.* II, xiv, 19–21)

[Furthermore, the Empyrean Heaven on account of its peace resembles the Science of Divinity, which is filled with perfect peace; this science does not at all permit of the strife that comes from differences in opinion or from sophistical arguments, in virtue of the supreme certainty intrinsic to its subject, God. Speaking of this science, He Himself says to His disciples, 'My peace I give to you, my peace I bequeath to you,' as He gives and bequeaths to them His teaching, which is the science of which I am speaking. Referring to it, Solomon says: 'There are no less than sixty queens, and eighty concubines; as for young handmaids, they are past counting; but unique is she who is my dove, my perfect one.' He calls all the sciences queens and lovers and handmaids, but this one he calls a dove, because it is unblemished by strife; this he calls perfect, because it enables us to see perfectly the truth in which our souls find rest.]

The strife which characterizes the earlier cantos, which account for the present state of Church and Empire, does not appear to belong to this heaven. The Empyrean, in his peace, resembles the Science of Divinity, Theology, where conflict and argument do not reign because its Subject is God, and He is unquestionably certain. In giving his disciples his doctrine, Jesus also gave them His peace. 'My peace I give to you, my peace I bequeath to you.' However, as Divine Science is one because God is One, for this reason His doctrine gives peace; on the other hand, the human sciences that interpret this teaching are numberless, and strife reigns supreme among them. There are as many sciences as Solomon's wives and concubines: sixty major ones, plus eighty affiliated ones, while those derived from these cannot even be counted. Everyone has a different view of God, and where there are so many, there is uncertainty and there is strife. What is clear in Heaven, is not so clear on earth. Dante's description of the coming dawn at the beginning of *Paradiso* XXX can be read as an indication of how the certainty of Divine Science loses all certainty for man on earth:

> quando il mezzo del cielo, a noi profondo,
>   comincia a farsi tal, ch'alcuna stella
>   *perde il parere infino a questo fondo;*
>   (*Par.* XXX, 4–6; emphasis mine)

[when the midst of heaven deep above us begins to grow so much that some stars *are lost to sight at this depth;*]

The stars that are lost to sight from the earth describe the distance and loss of certainty from the Divine Science to the Human Sciences, which Dante makes clear in that 'parere,' which can mean both 'appearance' and 'opinion.' Our human sciences have only a distant resemblance to true Divine Science, just one opinion among many.

Another 'parere' concerns Beatrice, whose true beauty, Dante writes with tongue in cheek, can only be enjoyed by her maker 'suo fattor tutto la goda' (*Par.* XXX, 21). Of course, we are meant to think that the reference is to God, but since Beatrice's 'fattor' is really Dante, our opinion, 'parere' would be wrong. In fact, it is to the *Vita nuova* that Dante refers when he recalls the first day he saw Beatrice.

> Dal primo giorno ch'i' vidi il suo viso
>   in questa vita, infino a questa vista
>   (*Par.* XXX, 28–9)

[From the first day when in this life I saw her face, until this point]

But Dante also appears to be confessing his inability to do her justice poetically, and to be ready to give up describing her altogether:

> *non m'è il seguire al mio cantar preciso;*
> ma or convien che mio seguir desista
>   più dietro a sua bellezza, poetando,
>   come a l'ultimo suo ciscuno artista.
> (*Par.* XXX, 30–3; emphasis mine)

[*I have been unable to keep up with my singing*; but now it is best that, in poetizing, I desist from pursuing her beauty, as any artist must when he reaches the end.]

Commentators like Sapegno read these lines as an obstacle that stands in Dante's way of adequately describing Beatrice. The reason, of course, is that, traditionally, Dante criticism sees no difference between the Beatrice of the *Vita nova* and the Beatrice of the *Commedia*. Even when critics understand the later Beatrice as a symbol of Theology they still regard the first and the second Beatrice as really the same person. In *Reading Dante Reading*, I have tried to show that the Beatrice that appears in the famous prologue in Heaven is no longer the same Beatrice of the *Vita nova* but is now a poetic figure for the 'donna gentile,' or philosophy, that is, the figure of Dante's allegorical poetry whose true essence is poetic wisdom. From this perspective, the meaning of line 30, 'non m'è il seguire al mio cantar preciso,' does not refer to the difficulty the poet might have in describing Beatrice, but to the difficulty the reader may have in following close to Dante's poetic description of Beatrice in the *Commedia*. In fact, the reader will read 'suo fattor' of line 21 as referring to God, when Beatrice's real 'fattor' is Dante. In pointing to his role as poet and artist, Dante is stating that he will no longer speak of her beauty, as he has done so far, because now it is time to dismiss Beatrice and bring the poem to a close, 'l'ardua sua matera terminando' [bringing the arduous subject to a close] (36).

But Beatrice does not leave Dante before she has fulfilled one more task, which is to satisfy his desire to know and understand what he sees: 'L'alto disio che mo t'infiamma e urge,/ d'aver notizia di ciò che tu vei' [The high desire which now inflames and urges you to know what you see] (*Par.* XXX, 70–1). Although what Dante sees is a river of light, the river and the topazes that he describes are mere fictions or figures of what Dante wants to express: 'son di lor vero umbriferi prefazii' [shadowy prefaces of their truth] (78).

164   The Poetics of Dante's *Paradiso*

The reason behind Dante's drinking from the river of light is to be able to see the truth of what was hidden from him, which, in this case, is the duplicity of Clement V towards Henry VII: 'Poi come gente stata sotto larve/che pare altro che prima, se si sveste/ la sembianza non sua in che disparve' [Then, as folk who have been under a cocoon seem other than before, if they undo their semblances under which they hid] (*Par.* XXX, 91–3). At the time Dante wrote this canto Henry VII was already dead, and with him Dante's hopes and those of his fellow Ghibellines of a monarchy in Italy that could counter the ambitions and greed of the papacy. Henry VII's seat ('gran seggio') (133) is now vacant, but it will be soon occupied by his soul ('sederà l'alma [...] dell'alto Arrigo') (136–7). This event, however, does not imply the future coming of Henry VII, as is often thought, but his vindication by denouncing the blind greed of those who, unable to see through the deceit of pope Clement V, did not support him, thus jeopardizing their own freedom.

> La cieca cupidigia che v'ammalia
>   simili fatti v'ha al fantolino
>   che muor per fame e caccia via la balia.
> E fia prefetto nel foro divino
>   allora tal, che palese e coverto
>   non anderà con lui per un cammino.
> Ma poco poi sarà da Dio sofferto
>   nel santo officio; ch'el sarà detruso
>   là dove Simon mago è per suo merto,
> e farà quel d'Alagna intrar piú giuso.'
>   (*Par.* XXX, 139–48)

[The blind greed which bewitches you has made you like the little child who dies of hunger and drives away his nurse. And such a one will then be prefect in the divine forum who openly and secretly will not go with him along the same road. But not for long shall God suffer him in the holy office; for he shall be thrust down where Simon Magus is for his deserts, and shall make the one from Alagna go deeper still.']

Clement V's deceit, which was already denounced by Cacciaguida in *Paradiso* XVII (82), 'ma pria che 'l Guasco l'alto Arrigo inganni' [before the Gascon deceives the lofty Henry], finds its punishment in this canto. Dante's apostrophe to 'blind greed' also recalls the she-wolf at the beginning of the poem, who is the symbol of greed, as well as the Veltro's aim to denounce examples of greed and punish them. In this final judgment Dante fulfils the mandate of the DXV by uncovering the deceit behind the apparent goodwill and magnanimity of pope Clement V towards Henry VII, and to punish him by dispatching him to the deepest and remotest parts of Hell, this time in a kind of double *contrapasso*. By being punished in the hole of the Simonists, in *Inferno* XIX, Clement V, the 'pastor sanza legge' [the lawless shepherd] (83), will push Boniface VIII even deeper into the hole.

* * *

With *Paradiso* XXX we could say that the mandate of the DXV, to denounce and punish the Giant and the Thievish Woman, the Empire, and the Church, has been fulfilled. In *Paradiso* XXXI, with Beatrice's disappearance, Dante's guide for the next two cantos is St Bernard, who, as a devotee of the Virgin, gives an account, in *Paradiso* XXXII, of how the Blessed are ordered in the 'candida rosa' [candide rose] according to their degree of faith in Christ, and whether their salvation was based on their own merit or on the merit of others. With the mention of Lucy, the poem comes to a full circle as Dante recalls the events of *Inferno* II that made the journey of the *Commedia* possible:

> e contro al maggior padre di famiglia
>   siede Lucia, che mosse la tua donna,
>   *quando chinavi, a ruinar, le ciglia.*
>   (*Par.* XXXII, 136–8; emphasis mine)

> [and opposite the father of our family sits Lucy, who moved your lady *when you despaired, with bent brow.*]

Line 138 recalls the state of paralysis of the poet at the beginning of his journey, in *Inferno* II. Not believing that he was worthy to undertake the journey, as Aeneas or St Paul were, Dante thought it folly to head out on his own, or even under Virgil's guidance, without permission from a higher authority. Virgil, then, reveals that he has not come on his own free will but was sent by Beatrice, who in her turn was asked by Lucy, who was sent by the 'donna gentile,' who, as I have shown, is a reference to Lady Philosophy, and to the 'donna gentile' of the *Vita nuova*, who is the real authority behind Dante's *Commedia*; that is, poetic wisdom.[1] (For a more detailed discussion, see chap. 4 of *Reading Dante Reading*.)

When Lucy is mentioned in *Paradiso* XXXII, however, no mention is made of who sent Lucy, but only that she moved Beatrice, as if Lucy had 'moved' Beatrice on her own, and not because she was sent by the 'donna gentile.' However, as I have indicated in my reading of *Inferno* II, Lucy as the figure which empowers Beatrice is another word for 'allegory,' which moves Dante's poem by mediating between Beatrice, the figure of Dante's poetry, and the 'donna gentile,' the philosophical and moral implications of Dante's poetry. Allegory is the figure that gives authority to Dante's poem and makes possible the underlying meaning of Dante's poem. Now that Beatrice, or poetry, has disappeared, all that is left is Lucy, or allegory.

* * *

In *Paradiso* XXXIII, the final and concluding canto, Dante reintroduces the impossibility topos to underscore the impossibility of describing in human language the final Divine vision. 'Da quince innanzi il mio veder fu maggio/ che 'l parlar nostro, ch'a tal vista cede, e cede la memoria a tanto oltraggio' [From here on my vision was greater than speech can account for, which fails at such sight, and at such excess memory fails] (*Par.* XXXIII, 55–7). Dante compares the limitations of human language to the Sybil's pronouncements, which written on a leaf are easily dispersed by the wind:

> Cosí la neve al sol si disigilla;
>   cosí al vento ne le foglie levi
>   si perdea la sentenza di Sibilla.
>   (*Par.* XXXIII, 64–6)

[So is the snow unsealed by the sun; so the Sybil's oracle [written] on light leaves was lost in the wind.]

Dante also gives the example of the geometer who fails in his attempt to measure the circle:

> Qual'è 'l geometra che tutto s'affige
>   per misurar lo cerchio, e non ritrova,
>   pensando, quel principio ond'elli indige,

tal era io a quella vista nova.
(*Par.* XXXIII, 133–6)

[As the geometer who wholly applies himself to measure the circle, and finds not, in pondering, the principle of which he is in need, such was I at that new sight.]

Yet, more decisive for Dante's purpose seems to be the contrast he sets up, indirectly, with the figure of the Virgin Mary evoked at the beginning of the canto in St Bernard's prayer. In fact, what is not possible for the poet is possible for the Virgin Mary, who is the perfect example of how the human and the divine square perfectly with one another:

tu se' colei che l'umana natura
 nobilitasti sí, che 'l suo fattore
 non disdegnò di farsi sua fattura.'
(*Par.* XXXIII, 4–6; emphasis mine)

[you are the one who so ennobled human nature that your Maker *did not disdain to become your creature.*]

The Virgin Mary is an example of the child who becomes the mother of her maker, of the creator who becomes the child of his creature, of the human becoming divine, and the divine human. And she has also the power to do as she wills:

Ancor ti priego, regina, *che puoi
 ciò che tu vuoli,* che conservi sani,
 dopo tanto veder, li affetti suoi.
Vinca tua guardia i movimenti umani:
 vedi Beatrice con quanti beati
 per li miei preghi ti chiudon le mani!
(*Par.* XXXIII, 34–9; emphasis mine)

[Further I pray thee, Queen, *who canst do what you will,* that you preserve his affects intact. Let your protection vanquish human instincts. Behold Beatrice, with how many saints, for my prayers clasping their hands to you!]

A similar prerogative is given only to God, as Virgil implies in his warning to Charon, who refuses to take Dante across to the land of the dead:

'Caron, non ti crucciare:/ vuolsi così colà, dove si puote/ ciò che si vuole, e più non dimandare' ['Charon, do not fret. So it is willed there where whatever is willed is possible, and ask no more] *(Inf.* III, 95–6). Only for God, and now for the Virgin Mary, 'volere è potere,' to will and to do are one and the same. The purpose of St Bernard's prayer to the Virgin is principally to perform a similar miracle for Dante, to preserve intact his 'affetti,' his human sensitivity, so that he will be able to go beyond his human limitations, ('vinca tua guardia i movimenti umani'), and capture the final vision and fully translate it into language.

The presence of Beatrice, who also prays with the other blessed for this miracle, is important at this point because what is being asked by St Bernard is precisely what actually occurs in the case of a poet, and between the poet and his creature. As a poet, Dante is a 'fattore' and is at one with Beatrice, his creature; and, similarly, he does not disdain to become one with her, as Dante repeatedly states in the *Paradiso*. As a poet, he has the same power to do as he wills. Therefore, St Bernard's prayer, ironically, asks for those very same qualities and attributes that Dante as a poet already possesses. It should be possible for him, therefore, to accomplish as a poet the miracle that St Bernard asks the Virgin Mary to perform. In fact, in the final analogy of *Paradiso*, and of the poem, the poet's desire and will are said to coincide.

> ma già volgeva il mio disio e 'l velle,
> sí come rota *ch'igualmente* è mossa
> *(Par.* XXXIII, 143–4; emphasis mine)

> [but already my desire and my will were revolving, like a wheel that is *equally* moved]

Desire and will are said to be moving equally and at the same time, as commentators have often argued: 'Thus desire (of intellect) and will to attain (of "velle," a will that is both human and divine) emerge, at the end of this poem, as equally balanced as a wheel that evenly turns' (see Singleton's commentary to line 143). The analogy with the wheel tends to reinforce this reading, as the wheel of will and the wheel of desire move in unison. However, this is possible only if we are dealing with God or the Virgin Mary, or if we understand the example in abstraction, or symbolically, or as occurring in heaven, in which case the two wheels are concentric. But when we are dealing with man's will, or a man-made wheel, as in Dante's case, the reference is to the wheels of a cart, which do move at the same time but are always parallel and separate, never coinciding and never meeting.

Although in man's desire they always seem to coincide, will and desire are inevitably and intrinsically always separate, and no man or poet can ever bridge this gap. Even though it would be possible for a poet like Dante to make a similar claim, it would be an error of pride similar to Marsyas, and similarly punishable. As Dante reminds us, 'trasumanar significar per verba non si poria' [to go beyond the human is not possible in words] (Par. I, 70–1). Between man and God, the Divine and the human, stands language, and language cannot be transcended even by a poet of Dante' ability. Whenever in the *Commedia* this claim is made, it is always denounced as an error, and the error always betrays man's desire and his greed.

If Dante had claimed for his final vision the possibility of coincidence of desire and will, he would have fallen in the same error that he had written the *Commedia* to correct, namely, the possibility of climbing the 'dilettoso monte/ ch'è principio e cagion di tutta gioia?' [the delectable mountain, which is the source and cause of every happiness] (*Inf*. I, 77–8). The only 'vision' we can get at the end of *Paradiso* is an image of the poem that we have been reading all along, the *Commedia*, 'legato con amore in un volume' [bound by love in a single volume] (86), that is, an image of everything that is precarious and unstable in the universe: Man: 'ciò che per l'universo si squaderna: sustanze e accidenti e lor costume/ quasi conflati insieme' [what unfolds in the universe: substances and accidents and their relations, as though fused together] (87–9). And with an image of Man, we are also left with an image of the poet who is about to bring the poem to a close:

mi parve pinta de la nostra effige:
per che 'l mio viso in lei tutto era messo
(*Par*. XXXIII, 131–2; emphasis mine)

[it seemed to me depicted with our image: *because my face was entirely in it*]

It is only in this sense that desire and will coincide: the desire of a poet and his will to fulfil the intended task of the Veltro, and of the DXV, in Dante's *Commedia*.

Conclusions

Thematically, the *Paradiso* is not different from *Inferno* or *Purgatory*. As the punitive action of the DXV, announced in the last canto of *Purgatory*, this cantica continues the task that Dante had set himself at the beginning of the poem as the action of the Veltro to expose and denounce the greed in human nature, which is responsible for the corruption in the Church and in the Empire, if not in mankind in general. At the level of poetic representation, reading the *Paradiso* presents some difficulties, as its critique of the blessed souls is hardly noticeable. Dante compares it to the 'solco' [furrow] left by a boat when crossing a stretch of water. Although his target is always a character of some standing, as it was in *Inferno* or in *Purgatory*, Dante's main concern is with the general idea or principle the individual stands for, such as the question of justice in the Empire, the present state of the monastic orders, or, as in Piccarda's case, the issue of vows. Because one theme usually spans over three cantos, or one heaven, the traditional format of the *Lectura Dantis* is not very adequate for a discussion of *Paradiso*, as, perhaps, it was for the other two (although even in *Purgatory* the subject matter sometimes extends over more than one canto). A division in heavens is more appropriate because the description Dante gives of each heaven in the *Convivio*, in their analogy with the Arts and Sciences of the Trivium and Quadrivium, holds the key to the interpretation of the respective cantos of that heaven. Only by understanding this relationship are we able to read the 'solco' of Dante's critique and unveil the hidden 'flaws' of the blessed souls. These flaws are usually revealed through a series of cross-references, reflected images, or oblique references that Dante's writing leaves on the otherwise flawless and unblemished souls. As Folquet describes the mode of repentance in Paradise: 'qui non si pente ma si ride' [here we do not repent but we smile'] (*Par.* IX, 103). This is Dante's ironic smile that the reader can capture when he/she is prepared to read the cantica allegorically and ironically.

A reading of the *Paradiso* makes it possible to put into a better perspective Dante's other works: the *Vita nuova, Convivio, Monarchia,* and *De vulgari eloquentia*. As it relates to the *Vita nuova,* I have already indicated in my other study, *Reading Dante Reading,* Beatrice's new role in the *Commedia* as the intermediary of the 'donna gentile,' or Lady Philosophy. This new role qualitatively differentiates it from the aberrant love poetics of the 'dolce stil nuovo' of the *Vita nuova,* and is confirmed throughout the *Paradiso,* and in particular in Dante's examination on charity, where Beatrice's mediating role is made clear, together with the 'philosophical' objectives of his allegorical poetry.

Dante's critique of Church and Empire could not be a more radical departure from the *Monarchia,* a treatise where the Monarch is seen as God's appointed guide of the Empire and of mankind; where the Romans are said to be God's chosen people, and the Roman Empire theirs by divine right; where Aeneas is still regarded as a noble and magnanimous leader. Since we find similar conclusions in the unfinished *Convivio,* it is safe to state that *Monarchia* probably dates from around the same period. It is impossible to conceive that Dante could write the *Monarchia* when he has already castigated Aeneas and the rest of the Romans, together with Virgil, in the first canto of *Inferno.*

The *Convivio* has great relevance for the *Paradiso,* not only for the descriptions of the heavens but also for its poetics. As the mature work which marks Dante's new love for philosophy, it sets itself apart from the *Vita nuova* by establishing the bases for how to read the *canzoni* allegorically, and, eventually, the *Commedia*. In the *Paradiso,* the objectives of the *Convivio* are restated in the prologue cantos, in Dante's warning to his readers who are undertaking the reading of the cantica not to be seduced by the sweet rhymes of his poetry but to attend to the 'philosophical' meaning that his allegorical examples are trying to convey. As in *Convivio,* the error is still identified in the deceit inherent in symbolic language that promises the illusion of knowledge and of happiness.

In the *Paradiso,* in stating the impossibility of representing his vision of Paradise, Dante tells the reader to use his experience to read the examples he will provide: 'però l'essemplo basti/ a cui esperienza grazia serba' [let the example suffice for those who are graced with experience] (*Par.* I, 71–2). However, the term 'esperienza' must be understood differently from the 'esperienza' we associate with Ulysses, 'non vogliate negar l'esperienza' [choose not to deny [them] experience] (*Inf.* XXVI, 116). In the Ulysses episode the emphasis is on 'nostri sensi' [our senses] (115), on the sensual experience or pleasure to be gained from getting knowledge of new and foreign lands, 'del mondo sanza gente' [of the world without people] (117). This knowledge is deceitful, as is Ulysses' speech, whose siren-like 'dismal rhetoric' (orazion picciola) (122) leads his companions to certain death. The deceit is inherent in the claim that this experience will provide virtue and knowledge, 'virtute e canoscenza' (120), or, as '*lo filosofo*' Aristotle claimed, quoted by Dante at the beginning of the *Convivio*, happiness. 'As the philosopher says at the beginning of the *Metaphysics*, all men naturally desire to possess knowledge. This can, and should, be traced to the fact that every being has a drive inherent in its own nature directing it towards its own perfection: '*onde, acciò che la scienza è ultima perfezione de la nostra anima, ne la quale sta la nostra ultima felicitade, tutti naturalmente al suo desiderio siamo subietti*' [since knowledge is the highest perfection of the soul, in which our supreme happiness is found, we are all by our very nature driven by the desire to attain it.] (*Conv.* I, i,1). The knowledge that Ulysses promises his companions is the same that Dante, following Aristotle, promises his readers in the *Convivio*, a knowledge associated with man's desire for perfection and happiness.

In the *Commedia*, Dante takes his distance from this type of knowledge, and in the promise made by the Veltro, this aberrant knowledge is replaced with wisdom: 'Questi non ciberà terra né peltro/ ma sapienza, amore e virtute' [He will not feed earth or pelf, but wisdom, love, and virtue] (*Inf.* I, 103–4). To understand the importance of this shift from knowledge to wisdom we have to refer to Dante's other treatise on language and poetics, the *De vulgari eloquentia,* where, in discussing the 'vernacular' and the subjects most appropriate to the tragic style, which for Dante at this time is 'the highest kind of style,' he selects three themes: 'well-being, love, and virtue' (salus, amor, et virtus) (*De vul. el.* II, iv, 8). Dante, at this point in his career, favours the tragic style because his primary poetic model is still Virgil's *Aeneid,* where these subjects are amply and impeccably treated and exemplified. In fact, the term 'salus' (well-being) appears in the first canto of *Inferno* in the lines of Virgil where he extols the warriors who died, precisely, for the 'well-being' of Italy: 'Di quella umile Italia fia *salute*/ per cui morì la vergine Cammilla,/ Eurialo e Turno e Niso di ferute' [He shall be the *well-being* of that low-lying Italy for which the virgin Camilla and Euryalus and Turnus and Nisus died of their wounds] (*Inf.* I, 06–8; emphasis mine).

When, as a result of his 'lungo studio e 'l grande amore' [long study and great love](83), Dante discovers the true nature of Virgil's politically compromised poetry, as I have indicated in my analysis in *Reading Dante Reading* , he leaves unfinished the *Convivio* and the *De vulgari eloquentia*, and shifts his style from the high tragic to the lowly style of comedy, and replaces the illusory and deceiving claim of 'well-being' (salus) with wisdom (sapienza).

In the *Paradiso*, wisdom is referred to as 'experience': 'esperienza grazia serba.' As I have indicated, this is neither the experience of the *Paradiso* nor that of Ulysses; rather, and first of all, it is an experience of the deceit inherent in any promise of 'well-being,' or in any promise of knowledge, perfection, and happiness. The comic wisdom of Dante's *Commedia* consists, on the contrary, in the awareness of this deceit and of the self-deceit that makes it possible.

In the *Paradiso*, experience is related to reading the 'examples' (essemplo) allegorically, and is predicated on the ability to demystify the illusory claims of the symbolic language of desire (significar per verba non si poria). In the *Paradiso* this critical act of demystification is associated with 'ridere' [smiling], that is, with the comical or with irony, which defines this cantica of *Paradiso*, just as it does the rest of the *Commedia*, as an allegory of irony.

Index

Adam, 40, 43, 44, 74, 143–5
Aeneas, 40–2 , 47, 81, 83, 85, 86, 100, 141, 165, 171
Agapitus (Pope), 39
Albertus the Great, 63
Albumasar, 77, 78
Alighieri, Alighiero, 86–7
Alighieri, Dante: *canzoni*, 48, 49, 50, 80, 107, 126, 153, 171; *Convivio*, 9, 11, 13, 21, 48, 49, 61, 67, 80, 102, 107, 126, 148, 153, 154, 156, 158, 161, 170–3; *De vulgari eloquentia*, 144, 145, 171–3; *Letter to Can Grande della Scala*, 13, 14; *Monarchia*, 9, 11, 152, 155, 171; *Vita Nuova*, 49, 139, 162, 165, 171
Ananias, 141–3
Anchises, 81–5, 99
Apollo, 15, 16, 20, 87, 88
Aristotle, 60, 116, 117, 146, 147, 158, 172
Augustus (Caesar), 78, 83, 86

Barolini, Teodolinda, 12n
Beatrice, 3, 7, 8, 16–20, 24–7, 31–7, 43, 49, 85, 120, 126, 127, 136–8, 142, 143, 156, 162, 165, 166, 168, 171

Belisarius, 39, 42
Boethius, 63, 94, 154
Boniface VIII, 132, 133, 165
Busnelli-Vandelli, 46n, 136

Cacciaguida, 3, 10, 78, 81–108, 117, 125, 137, 164
Caesar, Julius, 40, 55, 82–8, 91, 99, 102
Casella, 21, 27, 44
Charles I of Anjou, 52, 53
Charles II of Anjou, 51, 52
Charles Martel, 10, 48–56
Circe, 150, 151
Clement V, 54, 164, 165
Conrad III, 92, 93
Constantine, 38, 113
Costanza d'Altavilla, 29, 30–3

Damiano, Peter, 117–19
David (King of Israel), 74, 113, 136, 138
Davidsohn, R., 86n
Dido, 46, 47, 55
'dolce stil nuovo,' 49, 143, 171
Dominican Order, 61, 64–8, 70–5
'donna gentile' (Lady Philosophy), 49, 138, 142, 154, 163, 165, 166, 171

Index

DXV, 3, 4, 6, 7, 8, 10, 11, 22, 54, 57, 58, 61, 75, 105, 120, 135, 137, 159, 165, 169, 170

Echo, 65, 66, 72
Empyrean, 4, 161–73
Esau and Jacob, 53
Euryalus, 100, 114, 172

Fiesole, 87, 100, 101
Fixed Stars, 4, 124–45
Florence, 57, 77, 78, 83–92, 95–106
Folquet de Marselha, 56, 57, 170–1
Franciscans, 61, 64, 68, 69–75, 121
Freccero, John, 14n
Frederick II of Aragon, 113

Grandgent, C.H., 50, 80
Graziano, Francesco, 63
Guelphs and Ghibellines, 38, 41, 88, 100, 102, 105, 110, 111, 133, 164
Guinizelli, Guido, 49, 143

Heaven of Jupiter, 4, 108–15
Heaven of Mars, 4, 77–107
Heaven of Mercury, 4, 36–45
Heaven of Saturn, 4, 116–23
Heaven of the Moon, 4, 23–35
Heaven of the Sun, 4, 59–76
Heaven of Venus, 4, 46–58
Henry VI, 29
Henry VII of Luxemburg, 7, 11, 164, 165
Herod Agrippa, 139
Hezekiah, 113
Hippolytus, 104, 105
Homer, 8, 83
Horace, 8, 14, 23, 24, 83

Iacomuzzi, Angelo, 13n
Innocent III, 69

Isaiah, 139
Isidore, 63

Joachim da Fiore, 70
John XXII, 111
Joshua, 56, 122
Justinian, 10, 38–44
Juvenal, 83

Kaske R.E., 7, 8

Latini, Brunetto, 101, 102, 107, 154
Lectura Dantis, 170
Liberal Arts (Trivium and Quadrivium), 4, 47, 170
Lombard, Peter, 63
Louis of Anjou, 53
Lucan, 8, 40, 83, 102
Lucy, 28, 151, 165, 166

Macarius of Alexandria, 120
Mars (God of War), 78, 91, 92
Mancusi-Ungaro, 7n
Matteo d'Acquasparta, 71
Mazzotta, Giuseppe, 4n

Narcissus, 25–7, 65, 66, 72, 155
Nero, 83
Nisus, 100, 114, 172

Orosius, Paul, 63
Ottimo, 29
Ovid, 8, 15, 19, 83, 104

Pagliaro, Antonino, 70
Parodi, E.G., 110
Pepin, Jean, 7n
Peter III of Aragon, 52
Peter Lombard, 138
Petrarch, 15

Piccarda Donati, 4, 10, 28–34, 170
Phaeton, 87, 88
Plato (*Timaeus*), 32
Pompey, 82, 83, 88
Primum Mobile, 4, 146–60
(Pseudo) Dionysius, 63, 156, 157
Ptolemy, 77, 78, 108, 116, 117

Quirinus (Romulus), 53

Rahab, 56
Raimondo Berengario of Provence, 42
Rhodope, 56
Ripheus, 114, 115
Robert of Anjou (King of Naples), 52–4
Roboamo, 75
Romée de Villeneuve, 42
Romualdus of Ravenna, 120
Rossellino della Tosa, 29, 30

Saly, John, 12n
San Victor, Richard of, 13, 63
Santa Chiara, 29
Sapegno, Natalino, 5, 21n, 42, 52, 63, 64, 70, 72, 87, 90, 110, 117, 150, 163
Schevill, Ferdinand, 87, 88n, 92, 107
Schnapp, Jeffrey T., 12n
Seneca, 77, 78
Siger of Brabant, 63, 70
Sinclair, John, 93–5, 107
Singleton, Charles, 5, 19n, 70, 80, 85, 86, 86n, 90, 100, 101, 105, 140, 151, 168
Simon Magus, 164
Solomon, 64, 72–4, 161, 162
St Anthony, 159
St Thomas Aquinas, 62–75, 146
St Augustine, 13, 63

St Benedict, 120, 121, 122
St Bernard, 13, 165–8
St Bonaventure, 64–6, 69–71
St Daniel, 13
St Dominic, 64–71
St Francis, 64–70, 122
St Gregory, 114, 156
St James, 125, 126, 135–41, 145
St John, 125, 126, 131, 136, 139–45
St John the Baptist, 78, 92, 93, 95, 96, 111, 135
St Paul, 13, 15, 85, 111, 127–9, 132, 141(Saul), 156, 165
St Peter, 3, 10, 58, 111, 122, 125–37, 145
Statius, 130, 131, 136
Sulla, 87, 100
Sybil, 166

Theseus, 104
Theodomir (Bishop of Iria), 140
Tiberius, 40, 41
Titus, 41, 43
Trajan, 113–15
Turnus, 40, 100, 100n, 114, 172

Ubertino da Casale, 71
Ulysses, 144, 150, 151, 154, 171–3

Veltro, 8, 10, 11, 14, 50, 61, 62, 107, 135, 165, 169, 170, 172
Venerable Bede, 63
Villani, Giovanni, 92, 101
Virgil, 8, 11, 40, 47, 82, 83, 86, 100, 102, 107, 114, 130, 131, 136, 138, 151, 165, 167, 171–3
Virgin Mary, 167, 168

William II, The Good (King of Sicily and Apulia), 113

www.ingramcontent.com/pod-product-compliance
Lightning Source LLC
Chambersburg PA
CBHW030323080526
44584CB00012B/677